T0196107

MACAT

An Analysis of

Elaine Tyler May's

Homeward Bound
American Families
in the Cold War Era

Jarrod Homer

ROUTLEDGE

Published by Macat International Ltd
24:13 Coda Centre, 189 Munster Road, London SW6 6AW.

Distributed exclusively by Routledge
2 Park Square, Milton Park, Abingdon, Oxon OX14 4RN
711 Third Avenue, New York, NY 10017, USA

Routledge is an imprint of the Taylor & Francis Group, an informa business

Copyright © 2017 by Macat International Ltd
Macat International has asserted its right under the Copyright, Designs and Patents Act
1988 to be identified as the copyright holder of this work.

www.macat.com
info@macat.com

Cataloguing in Publication Data
A catalogue record for this book is available from the British Library.
Library of Congress Cataloguing-in-Publication Data is available upon request.
Cover illustration: Gérard Goffaux

ISBN 978-1-912303-79-3 (hardback)
ISBN 978-1-912128-07-5 (paperback)
ISBN 978-1-912282-67-8 (e-book)

Notice

CONTENTS

THE MACAT LIBRARY

The Macat Library is a series of unique academic explorations of seminal works in the humanities and social sciences – books and papers that have had a significant and widely recognised impact on their disciplines. It has been created to serve as much more than just a summary of what lies between the covers of a great book. It illuminates and explores the influences on, ideas of, and impact of that book. Our goal is to offer a learning resource that encourages critical thinking and fosters a better, deeper understanding of important ideas.

Each publication is divided into three Sections: Influences, Ideas, and Impact. Each Section has four Modules. These explore every important facet of the work, and the responses to it.

This Section-Module structure makes a Macat Library book easy to use, but it has another important feature. Because each Macat book is written to the same format, it is possible (and encouraged!) to cross-reference multiple Macat books along the same lines of inquiry or research. This allows the reader to open up interesting interdisciplinary pathways.

To further aid your reading, lists of glossary terms and people mentioned are included at the end of this book (these are indicated by an asterisk [*] throughout) – as well as a list of works cited.

Macat has worked with the University of Cambridge to identify the elements of critical thinking and understand the ways in which six different skills combine to enable effective thinking.
Three allow us to fully understand a problem; three more give us the tools to solve it. Together, these six skills make up the **PACIER** model of critical thinking. They are:

ANALYSIS – understanding how an argument is built
EVALUATION – exploring the strengths and weaknesses of an argument
INTERPRETATION – understanding issues of meaning

CREATIVE THINKING – coming up with new ideas and fresh connections
PROBLEM-SOLVING – producing strong solutions
REASONING – creating strong arguments

To find out more, visit **WWW.MACAT.COM.**

CRITICAL THINKING AND *HOMEWARD BOUND*

Primary critical thinking skill: ANALYSIS
Secondary critical thinking skill: REASONING

Elaine Tyler May's 1988 *Homeward Bound: American Families in the Cold War Era* is a ground-breaking piece of historical and cultural analysis that uses its findings to build a strong argument for its author's view of the course of modern US history. The aim of May's study is to trace the links between Cold War politics and the domestic lives of everyday American families at the time. Historians have long noted the unique domestic trends of 1950s America, with its increased focus on the nuclear family, neatly divided traditional gender roles and aspirational, suburban consumer lifestyles. May's contribution was to analyse the interplay between the domestic scene and the political ideologies of American government, and then to build a carefully-constructed argument that draws attention to the ways in which these seemingly disparate forces are in fact related.

May's key achievement was to use her analytical skills to understand the relationships between these different factors. She the traced ways in which domestic life and US foreign policy mirrored one another, showing that the structures and processes they aimed for, while different in scale, were essentially the same. She then carefully brought together different types of historical data, organizing her study to produce a carefully reasoned argument that the American suburban home was in certain direct ways the product of the 'containment' policies that ruled American foreign policy at the time.

ABOUT THE AUTHOR OF THE ORIGINAL WORK

American scholar **Elaine Tyler May** was born in Los Angeles in 1947 and earned her degree in history from the University of California, Los Angeles in 1969. She studied in Japan while her country was engaged in the Vietnam War, which forced her 'to confront what it meant to be an American.' May explored this further in her doctoral research at UCLA, which focused on the emerging discipline of American studies. She is currently Regents Professor of American Studies and History, and Chair of the Department of History at the University of Minnesota. Her professional awards include a Fulbright scholarship and fellowships from both the National Endowment for the Humanities and the Simon Guggenheim Memorial Foundation.

ABOUT THE AUTHOR OF THE ANALYSIS

Dr Jarrod Homer took his PhD in sociology at the University of Manchester, with research focusing on American culture and Jewish artists of the mid-twentieth century.

ABOUT MACAT

GREAT WORKS FOR CRITICAL THINKING

Macat is focused on making the ideas of the world's great thinkers accessible and comprehensible to everybody, everywhere, in ways that promote the development of enhanced critical thinking skills.

It works with leading academics from the world's top universities to produce new analyses that focus on the ideas and the impact of the most influential works ever written across a wide variety of academic disciplines. Each of the works that sit at the heart of its growing library is an enduring example of great thinking. But by setting them in context – and looking at the influences that shaped their authors, as well as the responses they provoked – Macat encourages readers to look at these classics and game-changers with fresh eyes. Readers learn to think, engage and challenge their ideas, rather than simply accepting them.

'Macat offers an amazing first-of-its-kind tool for interdisciplinary learning and research. Its focus on works that transformed their disciplines and its rigorous approach, drawing on the world's leading experts and educational institutions, opens up a world-class education to anyone.'

Andreas Schleicher
Director for Education and Skills, Organisation for Economic Co-operation and Development

'Macat is taking on some of the major challenges in university education ... They have drawn together a strong team of active academics who are producing teaching materials that are novel in the breadth of their approach.'

Prof Lord Broers,
former Vice-Chancellor of the University of Cambridge

'The Macat vision is exceptionally exciting. It focuses upon new modes of learning which analyse and explain seminal texts which have profoundly influenced world thinking and so social and economic development. It promotes the kind of critical thinking which is essential for any society and economy.
This is the learning of the future.'

Rt Hon Charles Clarke, former UK Secretary of State for Education

'The Macat analyses provide immediate access to the critical conversation surrounding the books that have shaped their respective discipline, which will make them an invaluable resource to all of those, students and teachers, working in the field.'

Professor William Tronzo, University of California at San Diego

WAYS IN TO THE TEXT

KEY POINTS

- Elaine Tyler May is a highly respected American studies*
  scholar whose works investigate the intersections of
  gender, sexuality, domestic culture, and politics in the
  United States of the twentieth century ("American studies"
  is a field of scholarship that examines US history, culture,
  politics, economics, and identity).

- *Homeward Bound* centers on how certain issues
  surrounding the Cold War* (a period of economic, military,
  political, and ideological antagonism between the United
  States and the Soviet Union,* and their allies) related to
  suburban domestic life in the United States in the mid-
  twentieth century.

- A key study linking US domestic culture to US foreign
  policy and the Cold War, *Homeward Bound* helped readers
  to better understand both of these areas and the United
  States' mid-century experience more generally.

Who Is Elaine Tyler May?

Elaine Tyler May, the author of *Homeward Bound: American Families in
the Cold War Era* (1988), studied history at the University of California
from the mid-1960s to 1975. She received her bachelor's degree in
history in 1969 and her master's and PhD in United States history in

1970 and 1975. A distinguished academic, May became a professor of American studies and history at the University of Minnesota; she has earned many professional awards, including a Fulbright scholarship, a National Endowment for the Humanities Fellowship (2013–14), and, in 2015, a John Simon Guggenheim Memorial Foundation Fellowship. She currently serves as the president of the Organization of American Historians.

May's work focuses on the relationship between personal and public environments. Looking at "private" experiences such as relationships, leisure activities, work patterns, and consumerism* (the ideology of material consumption: spending and shopping), she analyzes how they interact with political, social, economic, and cultural climates. May also investigates the intersection between domestic culture and wider social identity, specifically focusing on gender and women's experience in twentieth-century America. Her current research project, "Gimme Shelter: The Quest for Security in America," explores the quest for freedom in all its guises within American society.

Homeward Bound remains May's best-known work. Her continued expertise in the discipline of American studies has only bolstered its reputation.

What Does *Homeward Bound* Say?

US foreign policy during the Cold War of 1947–91 focused on "containment": confining the spread of communism and the influence of the Soviet Union, largely through the provision of military, political, and financial support to countries and militias threatened by or fighting communism. The term had many resonances in twentieth-century America, extending even to the domestic sphere as Americans spent the two decades following the 1945 victory in World War II* marrying young, flocking to the suburbs, and creating a baby boom* (a sudden increase in the birth rate). In *Homeward Bound*, May became the first scholar to establish a link between those two phenomena. The study's conclusions provide important clues to understanding American cultural history and the impact political policy can have on everyday life, while serving to enhance our understanding of women's history.

May shows how the "demographic explosion in the American family represented a temporary disruption of long term trends."[1] Divorce rates and the average age for marriage had been trending higher before the war while birth rates had been dropping. We may trace these phenomena to the cultural upheaval and demographic fluidity brought about by both the catastrophic economic downturn of the 1930s known as the Great Depression* and World War II, which began at the end of that decade. But this quirk of American culture in the 1950s reversed the trends for marriage, childbirth, and divorce. May shows how the husbands and wives of 1950s suburbia* differed both from their parents and from their own children—who would form the politically active counterculture of the 1960s. Both the prewar generation and the countercultural generation belonged to similarly progressive periods of US cultural history, with attitudes toward politics, sex, and culture differing sharply from those of their counterparts in the 1950s.

Homeward Bound challenges common assumptions about the political culture and the domestic climate* in America throughout the 1950s ("domestic climate" here refers to the culture and experience of home and family life, affecting things such as the roles of family members, gender norms within the home, leisure pursuits, and how the family relates to the community). The myth of the 1950s as a period of material abundance, consumer overindulgence, happy housewives, and suburban bliss was common at the time. And it has proven difficult to shake. One of the reasons May's work has attained such renown is that her analysis was one of the first to debunk these myths. Her analysis addresses the intertwining issues of sexuality, contraception, and marriage. She presents birth control as a facilitator of early marriage rather than something exclusively associated with the sexually charged 1960s and shows how popular culture*—the popular films, literature, plays, television, and so on, usually considered representative of a nation's attitudes and ideologies—in the 1950s actively encouraged women (once safely married) to assume a sexual identity within their marriage. Within this culture, sex was viewed as an important factor within the suburbs—which is at odds with the common image of sexually repressed suburban housewives at that time.

Overall, May offers a view of the 1950s as an era of evolution in terms of eroticism, birth control, and sexuality—things commonly believed to have been unacceptable to the American psyche of the time, but now unmasked as an integral part of the generation's marriage and procreation habits.

May draws on a wide range of source materials to produce a deep analysis of American culture in the 1950s. *Homeward Bound* paints a picture of 1950s America tainted with capitalist* and patriarchal* obligations that shatters the idea of domestic harmony so many associate with American identity and experience during this period; "capitalism" here refers to the economic system dominant in the West and founded on the pursuit of private profit; "patriarchal" refers to a system of male dominance with notable social consequences.

Why Does *Homeward Bound* Matter?

The title of Elaine Tyler May's *Homeward Bound* can be read two ways. It can evoke the direction that daily life took in the 1950s, with breadwinning husbands returning at the end of the day to their stay-at-home wives and suburban ideals. But it also evokes the cultural constraints of the time—the suburban home contained its inhabitants not just physically; it also represented a specific model of identity defined as distinctly American, supposedly democratic, and self-consciously traditional, conservative,* and patriarchal. The clever wordplay of the title subtly articulates the main focus of the author's study. First published in 1988, the work was reissued in 1999 and 2008, illustrating its continued significance.

As a piece of social history, *Homeward Bound* brings historical understanding into a dialogue with cultural analysis. May's analysis shines a light on the experience of women, both married and unmarried, reflecting the importance of women's history to May's academic interests. It also acknowledges the ways in which men were similarly constrained—in the workplace at least—by new "scientific" theories of management that left the home as the only remaining arena in which ordinary, hard-working men could assert control. And assert it they did: in the 1950s, the family dwelling and the women inside it became the ultimate symbol of certain political and ideological pressures.

May articulates the relationship between the political climate and the domestic sphere. In showing that the suburban home of the 1950s contained threats to the political and social fabric of the nation, she has created a study that remains relevant to the present day. For example, we may use May's approach to better understand the connection between political and domestic experiences in the period following the terrorist attacks on the United States of September 11, 2001 (9/11).* During the "War on Terror"* that followed, US President George W. Bush* promoted foreign policy and homeland security measures that had significant impacts on the everyday lives of many—Americans not excluded. May's study remains useful to anyone wishing to understand how American culture creates a reciprocal (two-way) relationship between politics and everyday domestic experience.

NOTES

1   Elaine Tyler May, *Homeward Bound: American Families in the Cold War Era* (New York: Basic Books, 1988), 6.

SECTION 1
INFLUENCES

MODULE 1
THE AUTHOR AND THE
HISTORICAL CONTEXT

KEY POINTS

- *Homeward Bound* persuasively illustrates how the political climate of the Cold War* impacted domestic life in America.

- Elaine Tyler May has been a highly respected American historian and a scholar of American studies* since the 1970s.

- May's pioneering study seeks to understand the role of women and the intricacies of the domestic sphere.

Why Read This Text?

Elaine Tyler May's *Homeward Bound: American Families in the Cold War Era* (1988) explains the political and cultural reasons that drove American people in the period following World War II to the suburbs to live a life of clearly defined gender roles in a nuclear family—two heterosexual parents and their children. May's study opened up the home and the sphere of domesticity*—home and family life—as an important arena of interest. She also demonstrated how scholars might use research in this area to better understand the historical cultural climate of 1950s America.

Appearances and conventional wisdom held that the abundance of consumer goods, apparent familial contentment, and the culture based on community values that characterized the suburbs arose spontaneously due to the nature of the American family. However, May demonstrated that it was in fact related to the tense political climate of the times.

> **66** *Homeward Bound* comes as a timely antidote to
> any nostalgia for the 'affluent' '50s or a revival of its
> domestic ideology. **99**
>
> Review, *San Francisco Review of Books*

The same ideology that urged a foreign policy of containment*—the effort to neutralize the political and military influence of the Soviet Union*—underscored the cultural atmosphere, promoting the social importance of marrying young, staying married, and having children while living in a suburban home well stocked with material possessions. For May, the government and popular culture* established the home, the exclusive province of the heterosexual nuclear family, as a bulwark against anything that might challenge the American way of life—a continuation into the domestic sphere of the foreign policy of containment.

This "American way" excluded not only communism*—the political ideology of the Soviet Union—but also homosexuality, extramarital sex, and everything else perceived as distinctly un-American. By these "American standards," the home became a place that subjugated women; the role of "wife" centered on continuing an American ideal.

Author's Life

Elaine Tyler May studied at the University of California, Los Angeles during the mid-1960s, earning an undergraduate degree in history, and continuing through to her PhD in United States history in 1975.

In 1968, while an undergraduate, May traveled to Japan to study for a year. She credits this experience as the moment that she became interested in United States history as an area of study. She told an interviewer, "Being in Asia in 1968 forced me to confront what it meant to be American, something I had never really thought about. It also forced me to confront the role of the United States in the world. So I returned home and dove into the study of US history in my senior year. As graduation approached, the field was just beginning to open up to me, and I knew I had much more to learn."[1]

May had originally wanted to pursue her interest in women's history through the discipline of women's studies.* But in the mid-1970s she found it difficult to find a suitable institution that offered the course or an available PhD supervisor. The disciplines of history and, later, American studies appealed to May because they allowed her to explore the areas of women's experience and American social studies. This helped her foster an approach that placed new emphasis on the relationship between the experiences of people's lives and larger social, political, and historical movements and events.

Author's Background

In *Homeward Bound*, Elaine Taylor May created a balanced and considered piece of cultural criticism. It benefits from her academic and informed approach, blending empirical data (information verifiable by observation), analysis of primary sources (documents and other forms of cultural evidence), historical insight, and archival research—essentially the result of May's vast experience as a student of US history; indeed, the main themes and issues at the heart of the work—gender, the home, domestic culture, politics, sexuality—typify May's entire body of scholarship.

In this historical study, May relies on a number of statistical and cultural sources to understand how political culture affected the representation of gender in the postwar era. The text examines the experience of Americans in the interwoven contexts of suburbia* and the home. It also takes a wider view of the cult of domesticity in the mid-twentieth century. May's considerable education gave her the opportunity to explore these themes in a groundbreaking piece of scholarship that changed our perception of American culture during the 1950s.

It is perhaps unsurprising that the academic community endorsed May's investigation into 1950s American culture from the outset; in writing her study, May enjoyed generous funding from a variety of academic sources, including the Mellon Foundation, the American Council of Learned Societies, and the Rockefeller Foundation.

NOTES

1   Interview with David Austin Walsh for George Mason University's "History News Network," accessed 27 November, 2015, http://historynewsnetwork. org/article/125031.

MODULE 2
ACADEMIC CONTEXT

KEY POINTS

- *Homeward Bound* is part of a longer scholarly investigation into the political and cultural atmosphere of the United States during the Cold War* (1947–91).

- Specifically, May's study is part of an attempt to examine how the social and political climate created by the Cold War and American foreign policy impacted the everyday lives of contemporary Americans.

- May added a unique voice to this academic debate, emphasizing the experience of women, and particularly wives, as well as the cult of the home and domesticity.*

The Work in its Context

Elaine Tyler May's *Homeward Bound: American Families in the Cold War Era* painted a novel picture of North American domestic life in the 1950s. Before her work, people accepted the idea that 1950s American popular culture* was conservative.* It encouraged traditional gender roles and attitudes toward sex and marriage, and it promoted the twin cults of domesticity and consumerism.* Scholars had also established the notion that the Cold War created an environment of anxiety, fear, and insularity in the postwar United States. Previous works by historians Paul Boyer* and Martin Sherwin*—*By the Bomb's Early Light: American Thought and Culture at the Dawn of the Atomic Age* (1985) and *A World Destroyed: The Atomic Bomb and the Grand Alliance* (1975), respectively—had already laid out that argument. So had journalist Godfrey Hodgson* in his book *America in Our Time: From World War II to Nixon, What Happened and Why* (1976).[1]

  66 Skillfully piecing together a social history of sex roles and mores [customs] governing dating, parenting, birth control, consumerism, and divorce from the Depression* to the late '60s, May supports her thesis with a wide range of unusual evidence, from Hollywood scripts and movie magazines to opinion surveys, economic studies, and federal employment and civil defense policies. Her larger aim is to dismantle the iron curtain that this culture (especially academic culture) has imagined between domestic and political events. 99

Constance Perin,* "A 'Herstory' of Private Life in the 1950s: Homeward Bound American Families in the Cold War Era by Elaine Tyler May," *Los Angeles Times*

Scholars usually regarded Cold War politics as somewhat removed from the domestic culture of abundance, prosperity, and contentment. May's innovation lay in showing the ways in which those politics in fact saturated American culture during the 1950s. She also demonstrated how the political policy of containment* curtailed opportunities within family and domestic life. In fact, it influenced every aspect of everyday American existence.

    May's investigation into the finer details of the conventional wisdom regarding 1950s US culture demonstrates the originality of her thought. So does her explanation of why social and domestic conservatism (based around conservative political values and nuclear family* units, comprising heterosexual marriage and children) emerged and gained importance during the postwar era. May connects the move toward containment and national solidarity in the foreign policy of the time with the more informal but nonetheless urgent cultural containment that emerged from the emphasis on domesticity and the suburban experience. In this way the book fits into a tradition of social history scholarship that began to develop in the mid–1970s and continues to the present day.

Overview of the Field

Many scholars before May had investigated the overarching political hostility of the Cold War. And some looked at how popular culture encouraged an image of the wholesome, abundant, and prosperous experience of suburban life. Elaine Tyler May attempts to synthesize those two views. *Homeward Bound* takes its place in the middle of a long line of Cold War social histories, preceded by texts like the historian Lawrence S. Wittner's* *Cold War America: From Hiroshima to Watergate* (1974). These texts examined a complex American cultural tapestry interwoven with US foreign policy and political imperatives.

By 1988, when *Homeward Bound* was published, scholars were thoroughly examining American postwar and Cold War history. Studies such as that by May's husband, the cultural critic Lary May*— *Recasting America: Culture and Politics in the Age of Cold War* (1989)— tended to offer broader assessments of Cold War culture.[2] May herself offered a more focused and precise analysis of the 1950s domestic climate,* looking at it through the lens of political culture. Her work gave scholars a more comprehensive understanding of the decade and allowed for a more detailed historical perspective, bringing into sharper focus what happened before and after the events and experiences of the 1950s.

Academic Influences

May's study sits comfortably within a more general scholarly movement of reassessing the Cold War. But one aspect of her methodological approach connects with both the contemporary climate of the 1980s—when May wrote *Homeward Bound*—and the interests of her study.

In both the 1950s (the period May is writing about) and the 1980s, popular culture, notably movies, reflected "traditional" attitudes regarding women and the home. The conservative political and cultural climate became manifest in the eras' cultural products. May offered an analysis of how Hollywood cinema propagandized and reinforced traditional gender roles, extending the foreign policy of containment to the domestic sphere. We can see this echoed in the way that American film promoted masculine ideals in the 1980s, especially as an embodiment of national machismo* (assertive pride in one's masculine characteristics). Movies in the 1950s that she mentions are *Niagara* (1953) and *Kiss Me Deadly* (1955). Movies from the 1980s are *Terminator* (1984), *Die Hard* (1988), and *First Blood* (1982). May's identification of these similarities between the 1950s and the 1980s makes *Homeward Bound* a timely piece of scholarship, if only perhaps by accident.

Homeward Bound analyzes women's experiences in 1950s America— and how those experiences were represented. So we may see this 1988 work as a late example of second-wave feminism.* That movement, which flourished from the late 1960s through the late 1980s, sought to improve circumstances for women; May frequently references studies focusing on women's experience, the home, motherhood, familial relationships, and feminism. *Homeward Bound* is a product of this cultural discourse (that is, scholarly and social conversation). May's study sought to understand the position of women in 1950s culture and how political and ideological imperatives dictated gender roles.*

NOTES

1   Martin J. Sherwin, *A World Destroyed: The Atomic Bomb and the Grand Alliance* (New York: Knopf, 1975); Paul S. Boyer, *By the Bomb's Early Light: American Thought and Culture at the Dawn of the Atomic Age* (New York: Pantheon, 1985); Godfrey Hodgson, *America in Our Time* (Garden City, NY: Doubleday, 1976).

2   Lary May, *Recasting America: Culture and Politics in the Age of Cold War* (Chicago: University of Chicago Press, 1989).

MODULE 3
THE PROBLEM

KEY POINTS

- *Homeward Bound* was part of a broad selection of studies that sought to better understand American social character and American popular culture* after World War II* and specifically during the Cold War* era.

- May did not set herself in opposition to any specific scholars or studies, seeking to create a more complex picture of the conventional wisdom about the postwar baby boom,* domestic experience, and suburban identity.

- May showed how suburbia,* birth patterns, gendered identity (the expectations and definitions of "man" and "woman"), and the emphasis on traditional and conservative* family values in the 1950s were intimately linked to American foreign policy.

Core Question

In *Homeward Bound: American Families in the Cold War Era*, Elaine Tyler May set out to discover how the cult of domesticity* developed such a firm grip on American cultural behavior and identity during the 1950s. Why did it become imperative that the roles of homemaker and breadwinner be so deeply ingrained within American identity? Why must these roles be so strictly divided along gender lines? Why was suburbia so strongly associated with socially constructed gender roles—and the origin of the postwar baby boom? And what did these large families in this family-oriented culture say about American culture and society as a whole? May sets out to explore why "in the cold war era, it was the vision of the sheltered, secure, and personally liberating family on which homeward-bound Americans set their sights."[1]

> ❝ In *Homeward Bound*, public policy and political ideology are brought to bear on the study of private life, locating the family within the larger political culture, not outside it. This approach illuminates both the cold war ideology and the domestic revival as two sides of the same coin: postwar Americans' intense need to feel liberated from the past and secure in the future. ❞
>
> Elaine Tyler May, *Homeward Bound: American Families in the Cold War Era*

"What," asks May, "accounted for the endorsement of 'traditional' family roles by young adults in the postwar years and the widespread challenge to those roles by their children?"[2] Examining private and cultural behaviors such as birth and marriage patterns and religious and leisure activities, May shows how the personal realm became linked to foreign policy and the conservative political and ideological cultural infrastructure.

Her investigation blended the existing scholarly understanding of the era's politics with the existing idea of the 1950s as a time of suburban bliss and nuclear families.[3] By examining these two aspects of US history together, May shows how political demands inspired ideological pressure to create family and community units impervious to outside ("un-American") influence. The political demand for containment* also limited opportunities for women, stunting political activism, ideological differences, and cultural diversity.

The Participants

In many ways May's inquiry was unique. While drawing on sources from a range of disciplines (film studies, women's studies,* cultural studies, history), her argument depended on preexisting scholarly knowledge of the era's politics and economy. Her study is part of a much wider line of inquiry about the American popular cultural experience during the Cold War era. But few studies discussed the connection between the foreign policy of containment and the shape of domestic culture in the United States.

May introduces her study in a way that suggests her thesis opposes widely accepted truths. At the very least, she explains, she will offer a very different impression of both scholarly and informal interpretations of gender, the home, and suburban identity in the Cold War era. As May puts it, referring to the catastrophic economic downturn of the 1930s known as the Great Depression,* traditional understandings "frequently point to the family boom as an inevitable result of a return to peace and prosperity. They argue that depression-weary Americans were eager to put the disruptions and hardships of the war behind them and enjoy abundance at home."[4] This same conventional wisdom proclaims the "1950s as the last gasp of time-honored family life before the sixties generations made a break from the past."[5]

While May never fully defines the "they" making that argument, she does provide diverse sources in her footnotes. She sought to offer an alternative to the existing understanding of the postwar boom in marriage and parenthood. She wanted to probe beneath the surface of mid-century American culture. The existing literature dismissed the home and saw the importance placed on traditional family values and gendered identity as an inevitable consequence of fear and prosperity; May offered an alternative view.

The Contemporary Debate

May's academic landscape was occupied by texts like Paul Boyer's* *By the Bomb's Early Light: American Thought and Culture*, Lary May's* *Recasting America: Culture and Politics in the Age of Cold War*, Martin Sherwin's* *A World Destroyed: The Atomic Bomb and the Grand Alliance*, and Godfrey Hodgson's* *America in Our Time: From World War II to Nixon, What Happened and Why*.[6] These studies all use broad methods of inquiry to examine both historical and cultural movements. But

Homeward Bound differs because of May's unique emphasis on interpreting the Cold War era through the lens of the home.

May's discussion of how domestic culture and the security of the family unit feed into wider sociopolitical concerns does not stand completely alone. It echoes a debate put forward by the American historian Christopher Lasch* in his 1977 work *Haven in a Heartless World: The Family Besieged*.[7] A contemporary review of *Homeward Bound* explains that "whereas Lasch lamented the passing of traditional family values and parental authority, May regrets the establishment of values that prohibited the growth of personal autonomy, particularly for women."[8] Lasch presents the nuclear family as the solution to the problems of society, as the starting point for a healthy cultural climate. In effect, May shows how propagating this belief serves to subjugate women, stunting individuality and restricting social diversity.

NOTES

1   Elaine Tyler May, *Homeward Bound: American Families in the Cold War Era* (New York: Basic Books, 1988) 18.

2   May, *Homeward Bound*, 8.

3   See Paul Boyer, *By the Bomb's Early Light: American Thought and Culture at the Dawn of the Atomic Age* (New York: Pantheon, 1985); Martin J. Sherwin, *A World Destroyed: The Atomic Bomb and the Grand Alliance* (New York: Knopf, 1975); Godfrey Hodgson, *America in Our Time: From World War II to Nixon, What Happened and Why* (New York: Random House, 1976).

4   May, *Homeward Bound*, 4.

5   May, *Homeward Bound*, 7.

6   Boyer, *By the Bomb's Early Light*; Sherwin, *A World Destroyed*; Hodgson, *America in Our Time*; Lary May, *Recasting America: Culture and Politics in the Age of Cold War* (Chicago: University of Chicago Press, 1989).

7   Christopher Lasch, *Haven in a Heartless World* (New York: Basic Books, 1977).

8   Winifred D. Wandersee, "Elaine Tyler May, *Homeward Bound: American Families in the Cold War Era*," *History of Education Quarterly* 29, no. 3 (1989): 498–500.

MODULE 4
THE AUTHOR'S CONTRIBUTION

KEY POINTS

- *Homeward Bound* looked at the complex reasons that mid-century Americans became so attracted to the ideas of marriage, parenthood, fidelity, consumerism,* and cultural conservatism.*

- Elaine Tyler May set out to move beyond the overarching historical approach to scholarship to create a clear understanding of the domestic experience during the Cold War* in 1950s America.

- May showed how the historical and political climate of Cold War America impacted the cultural and private sphere. In doing so, she created a convincing and useful connection between the two.

Author's Aims

Elaine Tyler May had two different intentions in writing *Homeward Bound: American Families in the Cold War Era*. On the one hand, she wanted to illustrate the connection between conservative foreign policies and the domestic climate.* She also intended to explore an American cultural environment that encouraged traditional gender roles,* cultivated consumer indulgence, advocated marriage, fostered a baby boom,* and promoted the suburban home as the bedrock of an ideal way of life.

We find May's key idea in the notion that foreign and public policy converged on the American suburban home. The family dwelling became a place where wider ideological imperatives were played out in a daily fashion by communities of settled nuclear families.* The home played a crucial role in translating the political policy of containment* into everyday life. As May puts it, "Within its walls,

> ❝ Her descriptions of family life ... have become a part of our conventional wisdom about the postwar era. In that sense, this study offers little that is new or controversial. Yet it does present an explanation—one that is well-conceived and convincingly executed. ❞
>
> Winifred D. Wandersee, "Elaine Tyler May, *Homeward Bound: American Families in the Cold War Era*," *History of Education Quarterly*

potentially dangerous social forces of the new age might be tamed, so they could contribute to the secure and fulfilling life to which postwar women and men aspired."[1]

May analyzes areas of 1950s and 1960s American culture and articulates the lived experience in suburban enclaves quite vividly. She accurately describes the tensions of suburban life for American families, detailing the deviancies and subversions that domestic containment supposedly repelled. The home becomes a safe haven from the ideologically and socially destructive forces outside. Domestic containment created a suffocating atmosphere though; the women of suburbia* lived a claustrophobic experience. May's work brought their reality to light in a new way.

Approach

May draws upon a number of sources to support her central argument and articulate the mood of the period. Of these, perhaps the most intriguing is the Kelly Longitudinal Study (KLS),* offering an excellent impression of how young Americans—particularly women, and especially wives—felt within the suburban home and nuclear family. As May argues, "The KLS questionnaires are a valuable source for finding out why white middle-class Americans adhered so strongly to a normative and quite specifically defined notion of family life at the time."[2]

May uses the KLS alongside other sources, including American movies that taught women how to behave, reflecting a positive prototypical image of the suburban home. She also draws on opinion surveys, gossip and movie magazines, economic studies, employment data, and political policies, tracing certain cultural elements, in particular those relating to defense policy. Some of these—especially those created and disseminated by the Defense Civil Preparedness Agency,* a government agency founded in 1950 to support the country's fight against communism—seem nothing short of ideological propaganda.

May opens the door to the 1950s family home by picking apart aspects of her source materials regarding suburban identity and the mid-century experience. In doing so, she exposes the tensions and limitations imposed by containment culture. But where did this culture come from? May begins by examining the cultural norms of the United States in the 1930s and 1940s—the years of the Great Depression* and World War II.* And near the end of her book, she gives us a glimpse into the future for her 1950s subjects as she discusses the ways in which containment began to unravel in the mid-1960s.

Contribution in Context

May's study aimed to offer an alternative assessment of the postwar boom in marriage and parenthood. As May puts it, in the traditional understanding of the period, both scholars and cultural observers "frequently point to the family boom as an inevitable result of a return to peace and prosperity. They argue that depression-weary Americans were eager to put the disruptions and hardships of the war behind them and enjoy abundance at home."[3] She points out that prosperity had similarly characterized the period following World War I* (1914–18) in particular, although without the accompanying increase in marriage and birth rates.

Many analysts, she notes, see the "1950s as the last gasp of time-honored family life before the sixties generations made a break from the past. But the comparison is shortsighted. In many ways, the youths of the sixties resembled their grandparents, who came of age in the first decades of the twentieth century."[4] By examining long-term historical trends, *Homeward Bound* portrays the period between the 1950s and early 1960s as out of sync with twentieth-century cultural evolution. Looking closely at the specific culture of this era, May offers up a different explanation for this cultural anomaly.

The work emerges from a solidly political and historical intellectual framework. Works like the writer Godfrey Hodgson's* *America in Our Time*, the historian Lawrence S. Wittner's* *Cold War America*, and especially the historian William Chafe's* *The Unfinished Journey* chart the developments of US politics and society in the Cold War but pay little heed to cultural evolutions and behavioral trends.[5] May personalizes this historical understanding by illustrating the impact of a top-down ideological structure where governmental behavior and policy impacts the everyday lives of ordinary Americans. This, May notes, explains why the generation that came of age in the 1960s pursued cultural revolution and political activism with such zeal.

Homeward Bound adopts some of the central tenets of an existing understanding of 1950s and 1960s America—specifically that it was the foreign policy of containment that drove the political culture. May also acknowledges the increases in marriages and birth rates, and the abundance and prosperity that abounded in the domestic sphere. But she connects these previously disparate aspects of the culture for the first time. And in doing so, she deepens scholarly understanding of this period. *Homeward Bound* allows the reader to see how the American experience in this era depended in part on a society-wide interchange of Cold War policies and American identity.

NOTES

1   Elaine Tyler May, *Homeward Bound: American Families in the Cold War Era* (New York: Basic Books, 1988), 16.

2   May, *Homeward Bound*, 14.

3   May, *Homeward Bound*, 4.

4   May, *Homeward Bound*, 7.

5   Godfrey Hodgson, *America in Our Time: From World War II to Nixon, What Happened and Why* (Garden City, NY: Doubleday, 1976); Lawrence S. Wittner, *Cold War America: From Hiroshima to Watergate* (New York: Praeger, 1974); William H. Chafe, *The Unfinished Journey: America since World War II* (New York: Oxford University Press, 1986).

SECTION 2
IDEAS

MODULE 5
MAIN IDEAS

KEY POINTS

- Significantly, Elaine Tyler May investigates how the experience of suburban families, and especially wives and mothers, embodied the political policy of containment.*

- May argues that the suburban home and all it contained became the embodiment of American capitalist* and conservative* ideals.

- May writes in a straightforwardly academic tone, developing her ideas through scholarly examination of the evidence, sources, and themes.

Key Themes

The overriding theme of Elaine Tyler May's *Homeward Bound: American Families in the Cold War Era* is containment. Specifically, she argues that the US foreign policy of "containing" the political and military influence of the Soviet Union* during the Cold War* in the 1950s and early 1960s carried over into the American suburban home. She sees that postwar Americans effectively practiced "containment" in many different ways: by their commitment to marrying young and staying married; by having multiple children; by moving to suburban communities where wives tended the home while their husbands worked hard outside of it; and by becoming ready consumers as they furnished the family home. For May, this informal cultural containment served to confine sexual deviancy and political subversion. It also limited opportunities for women in the workplace and hindered the development of individuality.

> ❝ More than merely a metaphor for the cold war on the home front, containment aptly describes the way in which public policy, personal behavior, and even political values were focused on the home. ❞
>
> Elaine Tyler May, *Homeward Bound: American Families in the Cold War Era*

May devotes most of her study to examining these forms of suburban containment. She finds it in attitudes about sex—including the role of birth control and the baby boom*—and sexual containment in the family home. She also finds it in the cultural representation of women, in understandings of the meaning of marriage, and in the new emphasis on consumerism.* May offers evidence about the plight of women struggling with the cultural expectations about womanhood. But the restrictions and failings of the era stand out most clearly in the experiences of married women.

Exploring the Ideas

May relies on evidence and sources that articulate how women themselves felt at this time, notably studies such as the Kelly Longitudinal Study (KLS),* conducted by the physiologist E. Lowell Kelly between the late 1930s and 1954, and on the portrayals of women in popular culture* such as American movies. Relying on films, advertising, and the general cultural milieu that encouraged the postwar ethic of success, May demonstrates that many elements of the culture worked together to model proper behavior for women. Movies analyzed by May include *Niagara* (1953), *Kiss Me Deadly* (1955), and *The Lady from Shanghai* (1947). She also discusses television programs like *I Love Lucy* (1951–7) and stage plays like *A Raisin in the Sun* (1959). May also marshals an impressive array of facts and figures to illustrate the details of the postwar labor force, spending, birth rates, marriage rates, and other pieces of relevant data; she then skillfully pieces the evidence together to describe the web of obligations and desires that entangled women and bound them to the home.

During the 1930s and 1940s, marriage rates in the United States declined and divorce rates increased. May demonstrates how these factors resulted, directly and indirectly, from societal upheaval and the increased presence of women in the workplace (although popular culture still maintained the pretense that a woman's place was in the home). In the wake of World War II,* Americans began to turn to their families to create a sense of stability. As the outside world (characterized by the Soviet Union and its ideology of communism*) became increasingly hostile, holding a capitalist identity became increasingly urgent for 1950s Americans. The family unit offered the ultimate in group membership, security, and acceptance.

May also shows how heterosexual marriage was promoted in the culture of the day as a defense against communism and social and ideological subversion. As this culture linked communism with sexual depravity, any sexual behavior outside of man-and-wife (and indeed outside of marriage) came to be seen not only as immoral but also as politically subversive and socially dangerous; people indulging in such acts were positioned as threats to the democratic ideal. So women were encouraged to satisfy their husband's needs—sexual or otherwise—within the home. Contentment here would discourage men from straying from the bounds of acceptable and safe cultural norms. As May puts it, "men in sexually fulfilling marriages would not be tempted by the degenerate seductions of the outside world that came from pornography, prostitution, 'loose women,' or homosexuals. They would be able to stand up to the communists. They would be able to prevent the destruction of the nation's moral fiber and its inevitable result: communist takeover from inside as well as outside the country."[1]

The culture also encouraged women to be consumers. First, the process of domestic consumption reinforced the culturally ingrained gender roles* of breadwinner and homemaker. Second, by furnishing and improving the suburban home, Americans demonstrated how successful the democratic, capitalist, American way of life could be. Finally, wives were especially encouraged to master what we might call "domestic survival skills." These included stocking pantries, rotating canned goods, and cooking. Coupled with the sexual righteousness of the heterosexual marriage, this established the suburban home as a symbol of safety and belonging.

Language and Expression

The intersection between America's political climate and its domestic culture forms the backbone of May's investigation. She discusses the complementary issues of consumerism, marriage and work patterns, sexual relations, suburban living, and child-bearing along this axis of domestic and political containment.*

The discussion of these cultural trends and societal issues both illustrates and proves this connection between the private and the public, the state and the individual. May's analysis of American popular culture and the traces of lived suburban experience brings to life the central notion created by the themes of political and domestic containment. She then uses this to articulate the study's critical perspective—namely, that the containment culture in the domestic sphere arrested women's progress and diminished opportunities for them in the wider world.

As social history, *Homeward Bound* combines historical understanding with cultural analysis. Its overriding thematic focus, reflecting an important strand of the author's academic interests, remains the experience of women, and particularly wives. But it also addresses the consequences of a hierarchical work environment that stripped ordinary, hard-working men of their power, leaving the home as the arena over which they could exercise control according to the patriarchal* standards of the era's culture. The family dwelling and the women inside it came to symbolize the political and ideological pressures of the mid-century.

NOTES

1   Elaine Taylor May, *Homeward Bound: American Families in the Cold War Era* (New York: Basic Books, 1988), 94.

MODULE 6
SECONDARY IDEAS

KEY POINTS

- *Homeward Bound* addresses the importance of sexuality and birth control in the 1950s within the context of healthy marriages, the suburban home, and the perceived need to uphold American ideals.

- May attempted to realign the presence of birth control in historiographical* terms (that is, in terms of its relationship to other historical studies and writings on the subject).

- The discussion of birth control and sexuality in 1950s culture may have been lost in the context of the wider and more general impact of May's study of the policy of containment* and American culture.

Other Ideas

In *Homeward Bound: American Families in the Cold War Era*, Elaine Tyler May undertakes the daunting task of binding together the parallel themes of political containment and domestic cultural "containment." With two major themes to explore—both separately and in relation to each other—May's analysis never really ventures into the realm of secondary ideas.

Some interesting aspects of May's analysis serve to support key areas of the work. These aspects enable her to develop a more nuanced understanding of the era's historical makeup. Chief among these is the notion of birth control.

Scholars have long understood birth control as a facilitator of the sexual freedom that accompanied the cultural upheaval of the 1960s and the movements for equality between the sexes. May demonstrates

> **66** Marrying young and having lots of babies
> were ways for Americans to thumb their noses at
> doomsday predictions. **99**
>
> Elaine Tyler May, *Homeward Bound: American Families in the Cold War Era*

that birth control played an important role in shaping domestic containment. Although oral contraceptives—"the pill"*—did not hit the market until 1960, effective contraceptive methods existed long before that. These methods allowed for properly planned families that were a "blessing rather than a burden," to borrow a phrase from one of May's sources.[1]

In a culture that frowned upon premarital sex, birth control also encouraged men and women to marry sooner, "even if they were in college or still economically dependent on their parents, because they could postpone the responsibilities of parenthood until they were ready."[2] Overall, the acceptance and endorsement of birth control during and after World War II* supported the need to secure young Americans within the sanctuary and sanctity of marriage. It also encouraged an administrated society that maintained a controlled population by managing it into ideal family units.

Exploring the Ideas

The subject of May's secondary focus feeds into the notion of early marriage and birth control. The 1950s are often seen as an era of social conservatism*—sexual and otherwise. But May's study shows how society expected young married women to be ready and willing sexual partners within marriages; referencing the Victorian* period of the nineteenth and early twentieth centuries, she writes that, "unlike Victorian mothers, who were expected to be reluctant sexual partners who tolerated sex for reproduction only, wives in the postwar era were recognized as sexual enthusiasts whose insistence on conjugal satisfaction would contribute to erotically charged marriages."[3] This all served to make heterosexual marriage a bountiful and satisfying enterprise, more likely to ward off any interest in subversive or perverse activity, whether sexual, ideological, or political.

These two areas of insight illustrate the richness of May's methodological approach and the study as a whole. For May, the devil is in the detail. She paints a vivid picture of a suburban home that served to contain society's anxieties about sex, population control, children, and the workforce—as well as the more troubling things these anxieties represented, such as the threat of communism and sexual chaos. May intends to show how domestic containment depended on the image of woman as both the bearer of children and a romantic partner with a willing but nevertheless controlled sexuality.

Overlooked

Scholars do not often mention the ways in which May shifts the generally accepted timeline of history. She demonstrates how events and movements usually credited to the 1960s, such as birth control and the encouragement of female sexuality, actually arose in the postwar period.

It is not as if May hides this aspect of the study: she devotes three full chapters to the issue of sexuality, contraception, and marriage. But her analysis does not fit the myth of the mid-century. She presents birth control as a facilitator of early marriage rather than as a tool that enabled the sexual revolution to flourish in the 1960s. She shows that in the 1950s, society actively encouraged women (if only married women) to assume a sexual identity within their marriage. While this is hardly a progressive position, it nevertheless conflicts with the popular image of a sexually repressed suburban housewife. As May argues, "Like labor-saving appliances, birth control devices could contribute to enjoyment at home and heighten the standards for domestic conduct. Both kinds of products, however, placed the burden of responsibility on women and rooted them more securely as the custodians of the scientific home."[4]

Overall May illuminates the 1950s as a progressive period in terms of eroticism, birth control, and sexuality, demonstrating how these played key roles in encouraging marriage and procreation. This runs counter to the popular idea of the 1950s as a sexually repressed period. May's study attempts to open up an era sealed by a cultural memory that simplifies, and mythologizes, certain truths.

NOTES

1   Quote from "How to Plan a Family," *Ebony*, July 1948, 13–18.

2   Elaine Taylor May, *Homeward Bound: American Families in the Cold War Era* (New York: Basic Books, 1988), 144.

3   May, *Homeward Bound*, 99.

4   May, *Homeward Bound*, 145.

MODULE 7
ACHIEVEMENT

KEY POINTS

- *Homeward Bound* creates a persuasive link between political and domestic containment.*

- The scholarly rigor of Elaine Tyler May's methodology— the method she employs in her research and analysis— enables her to thoroughly test and comprehensively prove her thesis.

- One factor clouding May's achievement is the study's perceived lack of diversity in terms of its subjects' race, sexuality, ethnicity, and class.

Assessing the Argument

Elaine Tyler May's *Homeward Bound: American Families in the Cold War Era* can often feel less like an examination of the relationship between national politics and everyday experience and more like an exploration of the nation's mindset as recorded through the peculiarly narrow scope of one of her most important sources—the Kelly Longitudinal Study (KLS).* This was a study conducted between the late 1930s and 1954 by the physiologist E. Lowell Kelly in which some 300 married couples answered questions on their relationship, family life, and general experiences in the United States.

The KLS itself has issues: it studied only a white, middle-class, fairly well-educated and largely Protestant* group (Protestantism being one of the two major branches of the Christian faith). This hardly represents a cross-section of American culture and identity. But the ideological and political climate May addresses affected Americans in different ways. African American people certainly had a different experience of

> 66 May's thesis is an intriguing one, and we should be grateful to her for taking seriously a decade too often sentimentalized. 99
>
> Joan Aldous, "Review of *Homeward Bound: American Families in the Cold War Era*," *Contemporary Sociology*

life in the 1950s to those of their white counterparts—in many parts of the country the races remained segregated by law. Likewise, a person's ethnicity, gender, relationship, or family status, and even the type of home they lived in, granted or denied them different types of privilege; May, however, drew conclusions based on data that reflect an exclusively mainstream model of experience.

It should be noted that May does not just use data from the KLS. In her use of the KLS data, she sometimes paraphrases the respondents' feedback at length. While the KLS study certainly provides insight into how one demographic subset experienced life in the 1950s, May treats this singular viewpoint as a universal explanation of how US political and ideological pressures affected the wider American experience.

May hints that the mainstream domestic culture she described in *Homeward Bound* represented an aspirational prototype—rather than reality—for all Americans: "What makes the postwar demographic explosion even more curious and remarkable is its pervasiveness across all groups in the society. Americans of all background rushed into marriage and childbearing, even though many of these newly formed families ... were excluded from suburbia."[*1]

Here May suggests that a study of suburbia is a study of wider American aspirations. For instance, although societal norms excluded African Americans from suburban enclaves, they were not excluded from the *ideals* that suburbia encapsulated. With this in mind, May crafts a study that thoroughly and successfully examines the mid-century home; the consensus appears to be that the inquiry's narrowness does little to dim May's achievement.

Achievement in Context

We may see *Homeward Bound* as the culmination of a certain way of thinking about women and domestic culture during the 1950s. In this respect it remains mostly relevant today as a kind of reference text. Scholars often use it to support the argument that mid-century American culture was geared toward conservatism.* This cultural atmosphere subjugated women, "demoting" them to the role of homemaker, both in the domestic sphere and in the wider culture. On the other hand, *Homeward Bound* also demonstrates how reductive (or simplistic) the scholarly view of the 1950s can be. For so long, many saw it simply as a time of housewives and working husbands living in white-populated, middle-class, and largely Protestant suburban districts. In this respect, *Homeward Bound* serves as a starting point for studies that attempt to widen our understanding by offering up a more panoramic view of mid-century America.

May's class-specific analysis excludes those who were not so well off or who differed from the norm in any other way. Many other identities and experiences remain conspicuous by their (near) absence in the text: homosexuals, bachelors, unmarried women, urban-dwellers, African Americans, Jews, Hispanics, and people of other ethnicities. May does mention some of these other identities, particularly the experience of African Americans in relation to suburbia. But she largely limits her comments to the already understood notion that suburban enclaves excluded them. "Other" identities never become part of an ongoing debate in the work, or enter into the author's core concerns and thesis. This approach dates the work badly, as current scholarship demands well-rounded, inclusive studies that consider a cross-section of experience and identity.

Limitations

Although May has no intention of fashioning a theory with universal applications, two aspects of the study might have wider implications. First, May looks at a variety of cultural "traces" through the analysis of primary sources, from films and advertisements to the responses given by couples in the course of the KLS. By turning to different sources, the approach may be useful in the analysis of cultures other than that of the mid-century United States. Accounts and artifacts (examples of cultural production) from any culture can be analyzed together to create a textured interpretation of that culture, revealing certain trends, experiences, and identities.

Second, we may also apply the central notion that some kind of relationship or connection exists between the political climate and the domestic culture of a nation or society in other cases; national and domestic experiences and interests may have dovetailed in many historical moments. May's approach can help us better understand the connection between political and domestic atmospheres and experiences.

May has put this idea into practice herself. In the 2008 revised edition of *Homeward Bound*, she added an epilogue relating to the terrorist attacks of September 11, 2001 (9/11).* As the United States embarked on the "War on Terror"* following these outrages, the country's cultural atmosphere and the everyday lives of its citizens became linked to the political and military approach taken by the administration of then-president George W. Bush* in both foreign policy and homeland security.[2] For May, this cultural climate had echoes of the Cold War.* In both eras, the culture encouraged Americans to celebrate a freedom-loving, consumption-driven societal identity. This analysis shows how May's study might help us understand the specific ways in which politics and the more widespread, day-to-day domestic experience exist in a two-way relationship.

NOTES

1   Elaine Taylor May, *Homeward Bound: American Families in the Cold War Era* (New York: Basic Books, 1988), 9.

2   May, *Homeward Bound*, 217–28.

MODULE 8
PLACE IN THE AUTHOR'S WORK

KEY POINTS

- Throughout her body of work, Elaine Tyler May shows an interest in the relationship between wider political and cultural environments and the personal and private experience of domestic culture.

- *Homeward Bound* typifies its author's scholarship in that it studies popular culture,* the home, the family, the political landscape, and, crucially, the experience of women.

- *Homeward Bound* remains May's best-known and most enduring work, establishing its author's place as an eminent scholar in the dovetailing disciplines of women's studies* and American studies.*

Positioning

Homeward Bound: American Families in the Cold War Era, Elaine Tyler May's second book, examines American life in the 1950s. In her first book-length study, *Great Expectations: Marriage and Divorce in Post-Victorian America* (1980), she analyzed an archive of over a thousand divorce court cases from the late nineteenth and early twentieth centuries. Divorce rates rose by 2,000 percent during this period, and May wanted to understand why. Like *Homeward Bound*, this earlier work used anecdotal and firsthand evidence to unearth the personal and cultural reasons behind widespread societal trends. As *Homeward Bound* did later, the text examines the relationship between private values and the public sphere. But *Great Expectations* also focuses on a time of change for women's roles in society and the changing dynamics of family and home life.

> ❝ The well-known importance of the nuclear family in the nuclear age [was] extensively examined by Elaine Tyler May in her pioneering and influential work *Homeward Bound: American Families in the Cold War Era.* ❞
>
> Hilaria Loyo, "It Came from the 1950s! Popular Culture, Popular Anxieties," *European Journal of American Studies*

In both studies, May shows that cultural expectations and social norms impacted people's personal choices. Women faced a lack of opportunity and fulfillment outside of marriage from the early to the mid-twentieth century. In both eras studied, the culture promised that women could only obtain contentment and security within the bonds of wedlock. May's two studies illustrate how the culture fed these trends of marriage, divorce, and the family. In this brief extract from *Great Expectations*, May discusses the concerns of mass media, the home, family, and women's sexuality and identity—much as she did in *Homeward Bound*: "Mass media combined with mass consumption to democratize the marriage market ... Given greater marital options, hopeful wives began to desire more than merely the security of a roof over their heads."[1] *Homeward Bound* looks at what forced and then kept young people together in the 1950s and early 1960s, while *Great Expectations* examines the pressures that tore them apart. But both works deal with periods that are out of sync with otherwise continuing cultural norms and historical development; both look at how societal pressures impacted the opportunities for and position of women in American culture.

Integration

The aspects of American history May investigates in *Homeward Bound* reflect the research interests she has pursued throughout her career. She addresses the same themes and ideas in many of her other works, from full-length books to conference papers and journal articles.

May's works generally center on or are in some way influenced by the experience of women in the twentieth century. Like *Homeward Bound*, May's other studies examine how people's private worlds and personal experience reflect and interact with wider political, social, economic, and cultural values and belief systems. That is, she looks at how things like sexual and familial behaviors, consumption practices, leisure pursuits, and home life influence—and become influenced by—a wider sociopolitical interchange of ideas and principles. In *Barren in the Promised Land: Childless Americans and the Pursuit of Happiness* (1995), May explores the history of childlessness in American culture and what this tells us about how sexuality and the family reflect changing American identity and experience.[2] Her 2010 book *America and the Pill*: *A History of Promise, Peril, and Liberation*[3] almost acts as a sequel to *Homeward Bound*. It describes the cultural and personal events of American women from the 1960s onward as affected by the birth-control pill. Indeed, the introduction sets the study up to begin where *Homeward Bound* left off: "At home, the nation was in the midst of a baby boom.* Couples married young and had children quickly. Yet American women were growing restless. They were eager for a reliable contraceptive that would free them from constant childbearing so they could take advantage of new opportunities opening up for women outside of the home."[4]

Significance

The main themes and issues at the heart of *Homeward Bound*—gender, the home, domestic culture, politics, sexuality—fit seamlessly into May's scholarship. These continuing preoccupations mark her body of work as unified and coherent. She has carved out a niche within the discipline of American studies that addresses issues of womanhood, the family, sexuality, and the home. She has also sought to synthesize these research interests with a wider understanding of American political history and culture.

This niche has been influential within the field of American studies. It has brought to light the significance of women's experience throughout the twentieth century and has helped push the discipline to incorporate an understanding of how the private worlds, environments, and pursuits of individuals dovetail with the public sphere and the political culture. A favorable review of May's recent study on birth control, *America and the Pill,* calls her "one of the best and most penetrating historians of family life and sexuality."[5]

May remains a well-respected academic, and *Homeward Bound*—a frequently referenced and highly influential study—is her most significant work. It brings her scholarly concerns together and frames the interests of her overall career in an exemplary manner.

NOTES

1   Elaine Tyler May, *Great Expectations: Marriage and Divorce in Post-Victorian America* (Chicago: University of Chicago Press, 1980), 67.

2   Elaine Tyler May, *Barren in the Promised Land: Childless Americans and the Pursuit of Happiness* (New York: Basic Books, 1995).

3   Elaine Tyler May, A*merica and the Pill: A History of Promise, Peril, and Liberation* (New York: Basic Books, 2010).

4   May, *America and the Pill*, 2.

5   Ruth Rosen, review of "America and the Pill: A History of Promise, Peril, and Liberation," *The Sixties: A Journal of History, Politics and* Culture 5, no. 1 (2012): 133–5.

SECTION 3
IMPACT

MODULE 9
THE FIRST RESPONSES

KEY POINTS

- *Homeward Bound* frames itself as an analysis of a certain aspirational model of identity rather than as a broad investigation into American experience at large.

- Criticism of *Homeward Bound* concentrated on the limited perspective offered by Elaine Tyler May's narrow analysis of white, Protestant* Christian, middle-class identity.

- Despite these limitations regarding source material, critics applauded May's novel methodology and analysis.

Criticism

The shortcomings of Elaine Tyler May's *Homeward Bound: American Families in the Cold War Era* have been apparent since its initial publication. The Kelly Longitudinal Study* (KLS), which provided much of the book's data on the attitudes and experiences of married couples of the period, sits at the heart of this criticism. One earlier reviewer, Susan Ware, captures the issue clearly: "*Homeward Bound*'s ... reliance on the [KLS] ... silhouettes several weaknesses. As May readily admits, the survey offers researchers a window on the experiences of only a fairly affluent subsection of the white middle class, leaving open to speculation the impact of race, class, and ethnicity on family values in the postwar era."[1]

Ware also points out a flaw in May's KLS data: the respondents were teenagers coming of age, and got engaged, married, and had children during the early 1940s rather than the 1950s. So the young Americans taking part in the survey had already undergone many of the life events that were supposedly so affected by the late-1940s and 1950s Cold War* culture.

> **❝** May's scholarship is superb ... *Homeward Bound* is a
> major addition to the literature on the history of the
> family and significantly enhances our understanding of
> American society in the 1950s. **❞**
>
> Joseph Hawes, "Elaine Tyler May, *Homeward Bound: American Families in
> the Cold War Era,*" *Journal of American History*

Many other contemporary viewers raised the same kind of issues that Ware did. Critics agreed that *Homeward Bound* succeeded in demonstrating that domestic and containment* cultures converged at an interesting and interrelated point. Still, they pointed out that the research suffers by the narrowness of its scope. One historian sums up this attitude: "The questions that remain are a tribute to the ambitiousness of May's project. Not only does she unearth a previously buried aspect of American society in the 1950s, but she attempts to show how connected private and public life were, even ... in an era of intense domesticity ... never again will it be possible to think of the 1950s family as 'apolitical.'"[2]

For the historian William O'Neill,* however, *Homeward Bound*'s problems go beyond the narrowness of its investigation: "May's difficulty is that she has no evidence to support her thesis, except that the Cold War and the domestic revival coincided in time. Being so thin, her argument is easily discarded, even, for most of this book, by the author herself. What remains is a somewhat random collection of facts, quotations, and observations bearing on family life in the 1940's and 1950's, with much of which historians are already familiar."[3]

Responses

Scholars usually criticize the broad strokes with which *Homeward Bound* paints domestic culture and suburban identity. But May never intended to fully illustrate the breadth of American cultural experience in the 1950s, and she makes this clear in her study.

May recognized that her methodology would permit only a narrow investigation. In fact, in the introduction to *Homeward Bound*, she predicted the criticism that would be leveled at the study, writing that "although the KLS sample included only a few individuals from other ethnic or socioeconomic backgrounds, it was made up of men and women who wholeheartedly and self-consciously attempted to enact cultural norms."[4] From the outset, May contended that her study excluded other identities because the KLS had contained no data about them. For its part, the KLS had only included respondents who represented the domestic culture the survey sought to represent. The idea framing this perspective held that all Americans aspired to the quintessential ideal of the suburban experience. Studying this mainstream identity and experience would allow us to fully understand the psyche—roughly, the "mind"—of the mid-century.

While this might seem a somewhat problematic, or at the very least simplistic, argument, May does fully realize it within the study. In doing so, she has created a bedrock for future scholarship to explore more diverse, unorthodox, or nonmainstream identities.

Conflict and Consensus

May spent several years researching and writing *Homeward Bound*, the process benefiting from the support of an academic community through countless drafts, edits, and re-edits. She had ample time to incorporate comments by her peers in creating the work, but once it was published she did not address further criticisms. Both May and the academic community see *Homeward Bound* as one component of a much broader scholarly investigation into identity in mid-century America. The limited scope of May's investigation does little to reduce the study's reputation and usefulness as a seminal analysis of the home and of gendered American identity. Indeed, studies continue to reference it decades after its 1988 publication.

May's study established a solid basis on which other studies could elaborate. This has allowed subsequent scholars to investigate identities excluded from *Homeward Bound*'s methodology and debate.[5] For example, in *The Apartment Plot: Urban Living in American Film and Popular Culture, 1945 to 1975* (2010), the cultural critic Pamela Robertson Wojcik* shows how the study offers *one* perspective of the 1950s American home: "While acknowledging that the 'traditional' family of the fifties represented a newly constructed ideal, without deep roots in the past, May nonetheless views it, and the suburban ideal that goes along with it, as overriding … [W]hile acknowledging the complexity and contradiction at the heart of fifties stereotypes … [May] does not open up alternatives."[6]

Wojcik addresses a more complex version of the 1950s American home, centering her study on the apartment, which allows her to address notions of sexuality, race, gender, creed, relationship status, and age.

NOTES

1 Susan Ware, "Book Review: *Homeward Bound: American Families in the Cold War Era*, Elaine Tyler May," *Signs: Journal of Women in Culture and Society* 16, no. 1 (1990): 173–5.

2 Leila J. Rupp, "*Homeward Bound: American Families in the Cold War Era*," *Pennsylvania Magazine of History and Biography* 113, no. 3 (1989): 509–10.

3 William L. O'Neill, "Homeward Bound: American Families in the Cold War Era," *Wisconsin Magazine of History* 72, no. 2 (1989): 151.

4 Elaine Taylor May, *Homeward Bound: American Families in the Cold War Era* (New York: Basic Books, 1988), 15.

5 I think here of texts like Douglas Field, *Cold War Culture* (Edinburgh: Edinburgh University Press, 2004); Margot Henriksen, *Dr. Strangelove's America: Society and Culture in Mid-Century America* (Berkeley: University of California Press, 1997); Stephanie Coontz, *The Way We Never Were: American Families and the Nostalgia Trap* (New York: HarperCollins, 1992); Mary Caputi, *A Kinder, Gentler America: Melancholia and the Mythical 1950s* (Minneapolis: University of Minnesota Press, 2005); Robert J. Corber, *Homosexuality in Cold War America* (Durham, NC: Duke University Press, 1997); Elizabeth Cohen, *A Consumers' Republic: The Politics of Mass Consumption in Postwar America* (New York: Knopf, 2003).

6   Pamela Robertson Wojcik, *The Apartment Plot: Urban Living in American Film and Popular Culture, 1945 to 1975* (Durham, NC: Duke University Press, 2010), 17–18.

MODULE 10
THE EVOLVING DEBATE

KEY POINTS

- *Homeward Bound* has been identified as one of the first feminist* readings of the period ("feminist" here referring to the intellectual, political, and cultural currents associated with the struggle for equality between the sexes).

- May neither participated in nor instigated a school of thought. Instead, she produced a study that could be used as a reference for discussions of domestic containment,* the home, and the experience of women.

- *Homeward Bound* established an authoritative interpretation of mainstream women's experience and US domestic culture that has been crucial to subsequent studies.

Uses and Problems

The historian Karen Dubinsky* identifies Elaine Tyler May's *Homeward Bound: American Families in the Cold War Era* as one of the first feminist histories about the 1950s. But we might better understand the text as the last word in what Joanne Meyerowitz calls the "conservatism*-and-constraints approach" to the study of women and gender in the postwar period, specifically the 1950s.[1] *Homeward Bound* would become the bedrock of future scholarly investigations, but it also established an authoritative and specific reading of domestic culture in the mid-century focused on the way American society denigrated women.

May's focused thesis secures *Homeward Bound* as a study that can be seen as the culmination of a certain way of thinking about mid-

> ❝ Elaine Tyler May has argued persuasively that postwar cultural imperatives for women were peculiar and aberrant, not traditional. ❞
>
> Joanne Meyerowitz,* *Not June Cleaver: Women and Gender in Postwar America, 1945–1960*

century Cold War* culture. Her work leaves subsequent scholars free to address entirely new areas of interest in the period. These might include the experience of women in the Civil Rights movement* and the labor movement,* or domestic cultures among people of color.

As a groundbreaking piece of scholarship, *Homeward Bound* has been mentioned in subsequent studies—for example, the historian Christina George's "Critics Scoffed but Women Bought" (2011) and the scholar Daniel Cordle's* *States of Suspense: The Nuclear Age, Postmodernism, and United States Fiction and Prose* (2009).[2] These citations demonstrate that scholars do not debate the validity of May's core study.[3] *Homeward Bound* most often appears as "exhibit A" in proof of the argument that previous scholarship neglected key areas of cultural and political history. This seems a little unfair, as May intended her study to have a narrow focus. *Homeward Bound* has undoubtedly given subsequent scholars a window on the middle ground or mainstream experience.

Schools of Thought

Homeward Bound has become such a formative text because it established a certain way of thinking about 1950s American culture. It focused on how political imperatives encouraged conservative* and consumerist* ideals, and how those ideas impacted the day-to-day domestic experience of mid-century Americans. May's study cemented a scholarly analysis of the contained and conservative suburban "ideal." Studying this aspirational prototype helped unlock an understanding of wider American preoccupations in the middle of the twentieth century about the home, women, and the different ways in which life was experienced according to gender.

One of the foremost texts to take its cue from this way of thinking is scholar Lynn Spigel's* 1992 work, *Make Room for TV*. In the 1950s, television was in its infancy. Spigel analyzes how this growing leisure activity impacted and helped shape American values and beliefs. Her study looks at how television perpetuated and encouraged a conservative ideology relating to gender, fashioned on the principles of patriarchy,* and an identity for women as child-bearing homemakers. Spigel writes that television was "welcomed as a catalyst for renewed domestic values."[4] She also echoes May's argument that domestic culture and gender identities in the United States during the 1950s differed from those that came before and those that followed. While we cannot say that May belongs to a school of thought, *Homeward Bound* did inspire subsequent inquiries. These later works used May's conclusions as a reference point for wider debate.

In Current Scholarship

Scholars cite May's study often, especially in addressing areas directly related to women and the home. Social science studies, studies examining the urban environment, and those investigating the representation of women in American cinema or culture have also referenced May. *Homeward Bound* acts as an authoritative reference of a particular time and a specific interpretation. Scholars can use it either as a counterpoint to a wider argument or in support of a similar thesis.

Of course, some scholars have criticized *Homeward Bound* as telling a one-sided story about women's experience and domestic culture. The scholar Marie Rowley discusses this issue in more depth in her 2012 essay "The Housewife, the Single Girl, and the Prostitute."[5] Rowley cites May's study as *the* influential text in creating the "containment model" to describe gendered experience in the mid-century.

While this model remains a relevant concept, Rowley notes that it represents only one strand of a wider discussion, illustrating how some historians choose to highlight the "pervasiveness of 'ideological underpinnings' of the gender conservatism of the postwar years" in their studies while others concentrate on how some women rethought the female ideal "by creating a version of heterosexual femininity that retained many elements of the domestic ideal … while adopting some independence and sexual autonomy." For Rowley, this latter model of femininity "may be called the modified domesticity or Single Girl model"—an ideal that was only "resisted" through the construction of what was considered a "deviant form of femininity."[6]

English professor Anna Creadick's* *Perfectly Average* (2010) shows the ongoing relevance of an analytical examination of conservative ideals, suburban identity, and notions of containment. Creadick's work probes the mid-century trend towards "normative femininity." This recalls May's analysis of the drive to establish a secured domestic identity for women in the years after World War II.*[7]

Scholar Carolyn Lewis bases her 2010 book *Prescription for Heterosexuality* on the notion of domestic and sexual containment. She elaborates on May's ideas about the central role that notions of feminine sexuality played in the making of the domestic ideal. Lewis argues that "Underlying this domestic containment was a commitment to what scholars have labeled heteronormativity*— the notion that the gender and sexual performances of heterosexuality constitute the only legitimate expression of self, desire and identity."[8] Lewis examines the ways in which medical practitioners contrived to maintain heterosexuality as "normal," in the process helping to maintain the passive feminine ideal that is the focus of much of May's own analysis.[9]

NOTES

1   Karen Dubinsky, "Heterosexuality Goes Public: The Postwar Honeymoon," in *Queerly Canadian: An Introductory Reader in Sexuality Studies* (Toronto: Canadian Scholars' Press, 2012), 349; Joanne J. Meyerowitz, *Not June Cleaver: Women and Gender in Postwar America, 1945–1960* (Philadelphia: Temple University Press, 1994), 3.

2   Christina George, "Critics Scoffed but Women Bought: Coco Chanel's Comeback Fashions Reflect the Desires of the 1950s American Woman," *The Forum: Cal Poly's Journal of History* 3, no. 1 (2011): Article 13; Daniel Cordle, *States of Suspense: The Nuclear Age, Postmodernism and United States Fiction and Prose* (Manchester: Manchester University Press, 2008).

3   George, "Critics Scoffed but Women Bought"; Daniel Cordle, "States of Suspense: The Nuclear Age, Postmodernism, and United States Fiction and Prose," *Review of English Studies* 61 (2010): 838–40.

4   Lynn Spigel, *Make Room for TV: Television and the Family Ideal in Postwar America* (Chicago: University of Chicago Press, 1992), 2.

5   Marie Rowley, "The Housewife, the Single Girl, and the Prostitute: Constructions of Femininity in Postwar American Historiography," *Psi Sigma Siren* 7, no. 2 (2012): Article 2.

6   Rowley, "The Housewife, the Single Girl, and the Prostitute," 4.

7   Anna G. Creadick, *Perfectly Average: The Pursuit of Normality in Postwar America* (Boston: University of Massachusetts Press, 2010), 83.

8   Carolyn Herbst Lewis, *Prescription for Heterosexuality: Sexual Citizenship in the Cold War Era* (Chapel Hill: University of North Carolina Press, 2010), 4.

9   Lewis, *Prescription for Heterosexuality*, 38, 41.

MODULE 11
IMPACT AND INFLUENCE TODAY

KEY POINTS

- Despite its limitations, *Homeward Bound* remains a key point of reference on the intersection between gender, sexuality, domestic culture, and politics.

- Scholars regard *Homeward Bound* as a complete study of domestic culture in the 1950s and still use it to shape interpretations and debates.

- Scholarly critiques of *Homeward Bound* point to the narrowness of May's inquiry, noting that the text only analyzes the home in terms of a distinctly white, middle-class, suburban, conservative* identity.

Position

Nearly 30 years after its 1988 publication, Elaine Tyler May's *Homeward Bound: American Families in the Cold War Era* has retained much of its relevance. Scholars of mid-century culture turn to it for a variety of reasons: as an investigation into the suburban experience; as an inquiry into the relationship between domestic culture and politics; and as a key text in the reading of women's identity and experience. Today the study can be understood as an important text for scholars in the field of American studies.* It contributes to the understanding of many areas of scholarly inquiry: US culture in the 1940s (especially after the Cold War* began), 1950s, and 1960s; the home; women's identity; and domestic culture.

Homeward Bound remains a foundational text. While the usefulness of May's study has not diminished, the contours of American studies have expanded in the years following its publication. Scholarly

> ❝ While acknowledging that the 'traditional' family of
> the fifties represented a newly constructed ideal, without
> deep roots in the past, May nonetheless views it, and the
> suburban ideal that goes along with it, as overriding. ❞
>
> Pamela Robertson Wojcik, *The Apartment Plot: Urban Living in American Film
> and Popular Culture, 1945 to 1975*

understanding of the 1950s has become more diverse. As each new
study paints a broader, more diverse picture of the era, the limitations
of May's inquiry have become more apparent. Still, scholars continue
to turn to the text despite the findings of more recent scholarly
inquiry. In addition to offering a particular interpretation of the 1950s,
it also presents a complex understanding of the ways in which US
foreign policy during the Cold War impacted the lives and experience
of American citizens and families.

May's study remains a regular on university reading lists, and it has
been republished and reedited several times since 1988. *Homeward
Bound* has made a valuable contribution to the reading of mid-century
American culture. In combining an interdisciplinary approach (an
approach drawing on the aims and methods of different academic
fields), deep analysis, and a wide range of source materials, May charted
a useful and successful methodological approach.

Interaction

Strictly speaking, *Homeward Bound* is not really part of an ongoing
intellectual discussion. Scholars do not debate the central tenets of
May's thesis. But various commentators within academia have
addressed them. The arguments May raised and the areas of American
culture she analyzed remain of great interest to scholars.

Homeward Bound does not actively challenge or transform existing
ideas. Instead, the text lays a foundation within the broader discipline

of American studies and the specific fields of gender and cultural studies. By interpreting the mainstream experience in the 1950s, May allows subsequent scholars to investigate and analyze how other domestic and gendered experiences deviate from this paradigm* (the intellectual framework according to which evidence is gathered and interpreted).

Many scholarly discussions of gender or the home in 1950s American culture mention *Homeward Bound*. For example, the scholar Christina George briefly cites *Homeward Bound* in an article about how French designer Coco Chanel's* 1950s fashions reflected the desires of American women. George writes that women "were expected to channel their increased sexual and economic emancipation into the family."[1] This use of May's text demonstrates one of its wider applications. Scholars often use the study to provide a simple, but largely unchallenged, interpretation of American women's experience in the mid-century. Recent examples of this include Stephen R. Duncan's essay about blonde bombshells, stardom, and the Red Scare, "Not Just Born Yesterday" (2014), and Jeffrey Oca's study of American football and the construction of masculinity in the context of Cold War politics, *Discipline and Indulgence* (2013). Chelsea Barnett exported the concept to Australia; her 2015 essay "Man's Man" analyzes the postwar representation of masculinity in that country's magazines.[2]

The Continuing Debate

In some respects we might see the brief and unchallenged citations of *Homeward Bound* as a "passive" application of May's thesis. More "active" interpretations of the study use May's approach, thesis, or conclusions to launch a wider (or at least a different) investigation into American culture. Scholars especially use the work when discussing the role of women and the notion of domesticity during the 1950s Cold War climate. Take, for example, the Canadian academic Karen Dubinsky.* She notes that while *Homeward Bound* executes its central thesis effectively, if "we remember only those who obeyed the rules—the people of the white, suburban, middle-class fifties—we miss out on how the normal and the abnormal helped to create each other."[3]

Dubinsky uses May's seminal study as a central reference point against which to analyze people who fall outside of the mainstream. As she notes, studying the "abnormal" can enhance our overall understanding of individual, domestic, community, provincial, and national identities. Indeed, we may extend that into the international arena as well, following May's logic and the global ramifications of the Cold War. This quest for just and equal representation and the search for a greater, more nuanced, and more comprehensive understanding of the mid-century motivates scholars to revisit and build on *Homeward Bound*'s thesis.

NOTES

1 Christina George, "Critics Scoffed but Women Bought: Coco Chanel's Comeback Fashions Reflect the Desires of the 1950s American Woman," *The Forum: Cal Poly's Journal of History* 3, no. 1 (2011): Article 13.

2 Stephen R. Duncan, "Not Just Born Yesterday: Judy Holliday, The Red Scare, and the (Miss-)Uses of Hollywood's Blonde Bombshell Image," in *Smart Chicks on Screen: Representing Women's Intellect in Film and Television*, ed. Laura Mattoon D'Amore (London: Rowland & Littlefield, 2014), 9–28; Jeffrey Oca, *Discipline and Indulgence: College Football, Media, and the American Way of Life during the Cold War* (New Brunswick, NJ: Rutgers University Press, 2013); Chelsea Barnett, "Man's Man: Representations of Australian Post-War Masculinity in Man Magazine," Journal of Australian Studies 39, no. 2 (2015): 151–69.

3 Karen Dubinsky, "Heterosexuality Goes Public: The Postwar Honeymoon," in *Queerly Canadian: An Introductory Reader in Sexuality Studies* (Toronto: Canadian Scholars' Press, 2012), 349.

MODULE 12
WHERE NEXT?

KEY POINTS

- *Homeward Bound* will likely continue to inspire studies that bring together an analysis of wider social atmospheres, gender representation and experience, cultural debates, and the home.

- Elaine Tyler May's study will likely remain an authoritative reference text for future studies.

- *Homeward Bound* created a convincing connection between the political climate of the Cold War* and lived experience in domestic culture. This has made it a foundational text.

Potential

Elaine Tyler May's *Homeward Bound: American Families in the Cold War Era* has featured in countless studies that probe American culture in the 1950s. These range from notions of the 1950s home and the experience of women in them to works examining the influence of the political climate on cultural experience. The historian Joanne Meyerowitz's* *Not June Cleaver* (1994) and Pamela Robertson Wojcik's* *The Apartment Plot* (2010) provide two notable examples.[1]

The differences and similarities between these two studies illustrate *Homeward Bound*'s role as a reference point for further investigation. Both works revisit the social atmosphere May describes in *Homeward Bound*. But the later authors read this climate differently, seeking to expand on May's singular notions of the home and the ways in which men and women experience their gender within it. Meyerowitz challenges May's thesis by examining the many roles women played in

> **❝**This current domesticity-mania is unique in that it signals a profound social change among educated progressive Americans. It's part of a shift away from corporate culture and towards a more eco-conscious, family-centric, DIY* lifestyle, a shift that has potential to change the American cultural and political landscape.**❞**
>
> Emily Matchar,* *Homeward Bound: Why Women are Embracing the New Domesticity*

1950s culture and the diversity inherent in female identity in the era. Wojcik investigates how the focus on suburban dwellings as representative of American cultural and domestic experience clouds our understanding of people's wider cultural experience in the 1950s.

Neither of these studies positions its investigation in opposition to *Homeward Bound*. But both show how scholars use May's text as a conservative* counterpoint to their own research interests. They redirect May's inquiry to look at cultural and domestic experiences lurking in the shadows cast by the suburban experience.

Future Directions

American writer Emily Matchar's 2013 book *Homeward Bound: Why Women are Embracing the New Domesticity* both borrows May's title and employs May's reading of the ways in which domesticity might relate to wider society. Matchar discusses the embrace of domestic culture in the face of a daunting economic, environmental, and political atmosphere in the early twenty-first century: "The draw of nostalgic domesticity is not surprising. We're living in scary times. The economy has been in the toilet for several years now ... Our neighbors are laid off, our friends have lost their health insurance ... The environment's a mess ... the food system no longer seems safe."[2]

Matchar sees a new "cult of domesticity" reshaping women's role in society. Like May, she draws on a breadth of sources and anecdotal evidence to establish an understanding of women's experience in the United States. Matchar's study proves that interest in May's ideas about domesticity and the home remains active. Scholars continue to investigate the role of women in society.

It is difficult to predict who might next take up the challenge of studying the politics of gender within wider cultural contexts. But we can safely assume that many will do so. Future studies will likely investigate small aspects of American culture and gender representation. The American academic Alice Casarini's* discussion of the recent *Twilight** film saga fits this description. She argues that the *Twilight* movies encourage female self-fulfillment by promoting a singular ideal of marriage and motherhood. Casarini writes of Bella, the story's female protagonist, "Rather than expressing dissatisfaction with her utter dependence on male characters and yearning for something more than her role as a homemaker and a future wife and mother, Bella is happy to let her life revolve entirely around Edward and surrendering to his ability to protect her."[3]

This analytical synthesis of popular cultural texts, gender representation, and social contexts that can be seen in Casarini's work shows us how May's investigation may guide future study.

Summary

Homeward Bound opened up the home and the sphere of domesticity as an important arena of scholarly interest. May showed that we might use the home—previously thought of as a strictly private space—to better understand the cultural climate of 1950s America. She demonstrated that the consumer abundance, familial bliss, and community spirit that characterized the suburbs connected with the fraught political climate—despite conventional wisdom to the contrary. In fact, the same ideological demands for a foreign policy and cultural atmosphere of containment* abroad encouraged a similar culture in the home. From this culture sprang the need to marry young, stay married, have children, and fill one's suburban home with material possessions.

May shows how the home acted as a sphere in which the heterosexual nuclear family* could be contained. This culture took root because of the urgent necessity to maintain an American identity. Just as urgently, the culture sought to exclude things perceived as un-American. In this environment, the culture subjugated women and promoted the role of "wife." More than just a dwelling, the suburban home served as the meeting point for forces necessary to perpetuate an American ideal.

The connection between all these aspects sets May's text apart. She draws an analytical line directly linking the role of women with the issue of containment in foreign policy, pulling together the complex fibers of 1950s America, creating a cultural tapestry that incorporates the home, domesticity, sexual relations, birth control, Hollywood movies, and anecdotal evidence in service of her original and straightforward thesis. Her persuasive study proposes that the domestic experience echoed and embodied the political idea of containment.

May created an interdisciplinary investigation that may be used to examine any identity, American or otherwise. Her well-founded and comprehensive research created a firmly established, if necessarily narrow, understanding of the era. Her detailed picture of mainstream American life helps us understand why this model of identity became so ingrained in the subsequent accounts of the 1950s. Future studies can build on May's work, instigating wider investigations into American mid-century culture, identity, and experience.

NOTES

1   Joanne J. Meyerowitz, *Not June Cleaver: Women and Gender in Postwar America, 1945–1960* (Philadelphia: Temple University Press, 1994); Pamela Robertson Wojcik, *The Apartment Plot: Urban Living in American Film and Popular Culture, 1945 to 1975* (Durham, NC: Duke University Press, 2010).

2   Emily Matchar, *Homeward Bound: Why Women are Embracing the New Domesticity* (New York: Simon & Schuster, 2013), 11.

3   Alice Casarini, "Twilight of the Grrrls: Stephenie Meyer's Rehash of the Feminine Mystique," in *Discourses of Emancipation and the Boundaries of Freedom*, ed. Leonardo Buonomo and Elisabetta Vezzosi, accessed November 27, 2015, http://www.openstarts.units.it/dspace/handle/10077/11623.

GLOSSARY

GLOSSARY OF TERMS

American studies: an interdisciplinary field of scholarship that examines American history, culture, politics, economics, identity, cultural production, and identity.

Baby boom: an era of increased birth rates often accompanying social upheaval (as after wartime) or economic affluence (as in post-World War II America).

Capitalism: a socioeconomic system based around the principles of free enterprise, individualism, and the private ownership of both capital and the means of production.

Civil Rights movement: the concerted and coordinated effort undertaken by African Americans throughout the 1950s and 1960s to gain equal rights, abolish segregation, and eradicate institutional and de facto racism.

Cold War (1947–91): a period of economic, military, political, ideological, and cultural antagonism between the United States and the Soviet Union and their allies. The antagonists stopped short of the full military action that would characterize a "hot" war.

Communism: a political ideology that relies on the state ownership of the means of production, the collectivization of labor, and the abolition of social class.

Conservatism: tradition and the acknowledgment of accepted social norms.

Consumerism: in the context of *American* consumerism, this refers to increased material consumption that drives and supports the economy and that is usually encouraged by advertising and social norms.

Containment: a political approach to foreign policy that seeks to neutralize and contain the expansion and global spread of communism. In practice it meant that the United States provided military, political, and financial support to countries that were threatened by or fighting communism. In the case of Korea and Vietnam, for example, the United States made active and aggressive moves to fight communism overseas with the hope of halting the spread of communist influence.

Defense Civil Preparedness Agency: a US government agency founded in 1950 to support the country's fight against communism.

DIY: abbreviation of "do-it-yourself," essentially describing the act of undertaking general domestic repairs and decorating yourself rather than employing a professional.

Domestic climate: the culture and experience that surround home and family life. This might affect the roles of family members, gender norms within the home, leisure pursuits, and how the family relates to the community, among other things.

Domesticity: the experience of life based around the home and family.

Feminism: the intellectual, political, and cultural currents associated with the struggle for equality between the sexes.

Gender roles: the idea of domestic and social roles being defined and divided by one's gender, as in the "traditional" roles of mother and homemaker for women and provider for men.

Great Depression: a financial crisis that affected America after the stock market crash of 1929 and which lasted until the end of the 1930s.

Heteronormativity: the idea that all "normal" or socially acceptable relationships involve one man and one woman.

Historiography: the study of the historical writings on a subject.

Kelly Longitudinal Study (KLS): a study conducted between the late 1930s and 1954. University of Michigan physiologist E. Lowell Kelly surveyed approximately 300 couples via a questionnaire at regular intervals throughout this period to collect data about their relationship, family life, and general experiences in America as a married couple with children.

Labor movement: an organized effort undertaken by workers to gain better working conditions and terms of employment.

Machismo: the notion of being very masculine and proud of one's masculinity.

9/11: September 11, 2001, the date on which suicide bombers hijacked four commercial airliners to stage a coordinated attack on the World Trade Center in New York and the Pentagon in Washington, DC. An additional attack was thwarted when a fifth airplane crashed in a Pennsylvania field.

Nuclear family: a family unit consisting of two heterosexual parents and their children.

Paradigm: the standard example of something; a framework or form that can act as a model.

Patriarchy: a social order and culture based around the superiority of men.

The Pill: shorthand for oral contraceptives.

Popular culture: the entirety of a society's cultural production (films, literature, photography, theatre plays, television programs, and so on), ideas, movements, ideologies, trends, attitudes, images, ideas, and fashions that serve to characterize it.

Protestant: Western Christian denominations that broke from the Roman Catholic Church in the sixteenth-century Protestant Reformation. Each Protestant denomination has a different organizational structure, but all deny the authority of the Pope.

Second-wave feminism: a movement from the early 1960s through the late 1980s that attacked and sought to remedy sociocultural inequalities such as the subordinate role the culture expected women to play in the workplace, the home, the family, and so on.

Soviet Union, or USSR: a kind of "super state" that existed from 1922 to 1991, centered primarily on Russia and its neighbors in Eastern Europe and the northern half of Asia. It was the communist pole of the Cold War, with the United States as its main "rival".

Suburbia: the social and cultural aspects of living in the suburbs, a geographical location within commuting distance of urban areas and city life. Suburbia tends to be associated with familial wholesomeness, heterosexuality, patriarchy, consumerism, and conformity.

Twilight: a series of films based on the fantasy novels of Stephenie Meyer.

Victorian: a historical period marked by the reign in Great Britain of Queen Victoria (1837–1901). It was a time of peace, prosperity, and massive industrial expansion in that country.

War on Terror: a conflict waged by the Bush administration and its allies in the Middle East (principally Iraq and Afghanistan) in response to the attack on the World Trade Center on September 11, 2001.

Women's studies: the academic discipline examining women's political, cultural, social, economic, and personal experience.

World War I (1914–18): The war was fought between the Allies (comprised primarily of Britain, France, and the Russian Empire) and the Central Powers (comprised of Germany, Austria-Hungary, the Ottoman Empire, and Bulgaria). Centered in Europe, the conflict involved the major economic world powers of the day.

World War II (1939–45): a global conflict fought in Europe and Asia. The United States entered the conflict in 1941. The war ended in Europe with the defeat of Germany and its allies and in Asia with the dropping of atomic bombs on Japan.

PEOPLE MENTIONED IN THE TEXT

Paul Boyer (1935–2012) was an American historian who gained his PhD from Harvard in 1966. He specialized in the study of religion and morality in American cultural history.

George W. Bush (b. 1946) was the 43rd president of the United States.

Alice Casarini is a scholar who teaches at the University of Bologna.

William H. Chafe is a preeminent American historian whose keys works include *Civilities and Civil Rights: Greensboro, North Carolina, and the Struggle for Freedom* (1981), *The Paradox of Change: Women's History in the 20th Century* (1991), and *The Rise and Fall of the American Century: The United States from 1890 to 2008* (2008).

Coco Chanel (1883–1971) was a French fashion designer and perfumer whose work and label remain influential today.

Daniel Cordle is a reader in English and American literature at Nottingham Trent University.

Anna Creadick is an associate professor of English at Hobart and William Smith Colleges.

Karen Dubinsky is a professor of history at Queen's University in Canada.

Godfrey Hodgson (b. 1934) is a writer and journalist who has written about American history and politics.

Christopher Lasch (1932–94) was an American historian and social critic whose works include *Haven in a Heartless World* (1977), *The Minimal Self* (1984), and *The Revolt of the Elites and the Betrayal of Democracy* (1996).

Emily Matchar (b. 1982) is an American journalist and writer.

Lary May is the husband of Elaine Tyler May, and an eminent scholar who specializes in the study of American culture. His books include *Screening Out the Past: The Birth of Mass Culture and the Motion Picture Industry* (1983) and *The Big Tomorrow: Hollywood and the Politics of the American Way* (2000).

Joanne Meyerowitz is a professor of history at Yale University.

William O'Neill is an American historian and professor emeritus of history at Rutgers. Key texts include *American High: The Years of Confidence, 1945–1960* (1986) and *A Democracy at War: America's Fight at Home and Abroad in World War II* (1993).

Constance Perin is a cultural anthropologist whose books include *Belonging in America: Reading Between the Lines* (1990) and *Shouldering the Risk: The Culture of Control in the Nuclear Power Industry* (2006).

Martin Sherwin (b. 1937) is a preeminent American historian who won a Pulitzer Prize for his biography of Robert Oppenheimer, *American Prometheus: The Triumph and Tragedy of J. Robert Oppenheimer* (2006).

Lynn Spigel is professor of screen cultures at Northwestern University.

Lawrence Wittner (b. 1941) is an American historian specializing in American foreign policy and peace movements. His extensive body of work includes *Rebels Against War: The American Peace Movement, 1941–1960* (1969) and *Resisting the Bomb: A History of the World Nuclear Disarmament Movement, 1954–1970* (1997).

Pamela Robertson Wojcik is a professor of the department of film, TV and theatre at the University of Notre Dame.

WORKS CITED

WORKS CITED

Aldous, Joan. "Review of *Homeward Bound: American Families in the Cold-War Era*." *Contemporary Sociology* 19, no. 3 (1990): 458–9.

Barnett, Chelsea. "Man's Man: Representations of Australian Post-War Masculinity in Man Magazine." *Journal of Australian Studies* 39, no. 2 (2015): 151–69.

Boyer, Paul S. *By the Bomb's Early Light: American Thought and Culture at the Dawn of the Atomic Age*. New York: Pantheon, 1985.

Caputi, Mary. *A Kinder, Gentler America: Melancholia and the Mythical 1950s*. Minneapolis: University of Minnesota Press, 2005.

Casarini, Alice. "Twilight of the Grrrls: Stephenie Meyer's Rehash of the Feminine Mystique." In *Discourses of Emancipation and the Boundaries of Freedom*, edited by Leonardo Buonomo and Elisabetta Vezzosi. Accessed November 27, 2015. http://www.openstarts.units.it/dspace/handle/10077/11623.

Chafe, William H. *The Unfinished Journey: America since World War II*. New York: Oxford University Press, *1986*.

Cohen, Elizabeth. *A Consumers' Republic: The Politics of Mass Consumption in Postwar America*. New York: Knopf, 2003.

Coontz, Stephanie. *The Way We Never Were: American Families and the Nostalgia Trap*. New York: HarperCollins, 1992.

Corber, Robert J. *Homosexuality in Cold War America*. Durham, NC: Duke University Press, 1997.

Cordle, Daniel. *States of Suspense: The Nuclear Age, Postmodernism and United States Fiction and Prose*. Manchester: Manchester University Press, 2008.

"States of Suspense: The Nuclear Age, Postmodernism, and United States Fiction and Prose." *Review of English Studies* 61 (2010): 838–40.

Creadick, Anna G. *Perfectly Average: The Pursuit of Normality in Postwar America*. Boston: University of Massachusetts Press, 2010.

Dubinsky, Karen, "Heterosexuality Goes Public: The Postwar Honeymoon." In *Queerly Canadian: An Introductory Reader in Sexuality Studies*. Toronto: Canadian Scholars' Press, 2012.

Duncan, Stephen R. "Not Just Born Yesterday: Judy Holliday, the Red Scare, and the (Miss-)Uses of Hollywood's Blonde Bombshell Image." In *Smart Chicks on Screen: Representing Women's Intellect in Film and Television*, edited by Laura Mattoon D' Amore. London: Rowland & Littlefield, 2014.

Field, Douglas. *Cold War Culture*. Edinburgh: Edinburgh University Press, 2004.

George, Christina. "Critics Scoffed but Women Bought: Coco Chanel's Comeback Fashions Reflect the Desires of the 1950s American Woman." *The Forum: Cal Poly's Journal of History* 3, no. 1 (2011): Article 13.

Hawes, Joseph M. "Elaine Tyler May, *Homeward Bound: American Families in the Cold War Era*." *Journal of American History* 76, no. 2 (1989): 656.

Henriksen, Margot. *Dr. Strangelove's America: Society and Culture in Mid-Century America*. Berkeley: University of California Press, 1997.

Hodgson, Godfrey. *America in Our Time*. Garden City, NY: Doubleday, 1976.

Lasch, Christopher. *Haven in a Heartless World: The Family Besieged*. New York: Basic Books, 1977.

Lewis, Carolyn Herbst. *Prescription for Heterosexuality: Sexual Citizenship in the Cold War Era*. Chapel Hill: University of North Carolina Press, 2010.

Loyo, Hilaria. "*It Came from the 1950s! Popular Culture, Popular Anxieties*," *European Journal of American Studies* [Online], edited by Darryl Jones, Elizabeth McCarthy and Bernice M. Murphy Basingstoke. Reviews 2012-2, document 14. http://ejas.revues.org/9872.

Matchar, Emily. *Homeward Bound: Why Women are Embracing the New Domesticity*. New York: Simon & Schuster, 2013.

May, Elaine Tyler. *Great Expectations: Marriage and Divorce in Post-Victorian America*. Chicago: University of Chicago Press, 1980.

Homeward Bound: American Families in the Cold War Era. New York: Basic Books, 1988.

Barren in the Promised Land: Childless Americans and the Pursuit of Happiness. New York: Basic Books, 1995.

America and the Pill: A History of Promise, Peril, and Liberation. New York: Basic Books, 2010.

Gimme Shelter: The Quest for Security in America. Forthcoming.

May, Lary. *Recasting America: Culture and Politics in the Age of Cold War*. Chicago: University of Chicago Press, 1989.

Meyerowitz, Joanne J. *Not June Cleaver: Women and Gender in Postwar America, 1945–1960*. Philadelphia: Temple University Press, 1994.

Oca, Jeffrey. *Discipline and Indulgence: College Football, Media, and the American Way of Life during the Cold War*. New Brunswick, NJ: Rutgers University Press, 2013.

O'Neill, William L., "Homeward Bound: American Families in the Cold War Era." *Wisconsin Magazine of History* 72, no. 2 (1989): *151–2.*

Perin, Constance. "A 'Herstory' of Private Life in the 1950s: HOMEWARD BOUND American Families in the Cold War Era by Elaine Tyler May (Basic Books: $20.95; 284 pp.; Illustrated; 0-465-03054-8)." *Los Angeles Times*, March 12, 1989. Accessed January 24, 2016. articles.latimes.com/1989-03-12/books/bk-1233_1_homeward-bound-american-families.

Rosen, Ruth. "Review of *America and the Pill: A History of Promise, Peril, and Liberation*." *The Sixties: A Journal of History, Politics and Culture* 5, no. 1 (2012): 133–5.

Rowley, Marie. "The Housewife, the Single Girl, and the Prostitute: Constructions of Femininity in Postwar American Historiography." *Psi Sigma Siren* 7, no. 2 (2012): Article 2.

Rupp, Leila J. "Homeward Bound: American Families in the Cold War Era." *Pennsylvania Magazine of History and Biography* 113, no. 3 (1989): 509–10.

Sherwin, Martin J. *A World Destroyed: The Atomic Bomb and the Grand Alliance.* New York: Knopf, 1975.

Spigel, Lynn. *Make Room for TV: Television and the Family Ideal in Postwar America.* Chicago: University of Chicago Press, 1992.

Wandersee, Winifred D. "Elaine Tyler May, *Homeward Bound: American Families in the Cold War Era.*" *History of Education Quarterly* 29, no. 3 (1989): 498–500.

Ware, Susan. "Book Review: *Homeward Bound: American Families in the Cold War Era*, Elaine Tyler May." *Signs: Journal of Women in Culture and Society* 16, no. 1 (1990): 173–5.

Wittner, Lawrence S. *Cold War America: From Hiroshima to Watergate.* New York: Praeger, 1974.

Wojcik, Pamela Robertson. *The Apartment Plot: Urban Living in American Film and Popular Culture, 1945 to 1975.* Durham, NC: Duke University Press, 2010.

THE MACAT LIBRARY
BY DISCIPLINE

AFRICANA STUDIES

Chinua Achebe's *An Image of Africa: Racism in Conrad's Heart of Darkness*
W. E. B. Du Bois's *The Souls of Black Folk*
Zora Neale Huston's *Characteristics of Negro Expression*
Martin Luther King Jr's *Why We Can't Wait*
Toni Morrison's *Playing in the Dark: Whiteness in the American Literary Imagination*

ANTHROPOLOGY

Arjun Appadurai's *Modernity at Large: Cultural Dimensions of Globalisation*
Philippe Ariès's *Centuries of Childhood*
Franz Boas's *Race, Language and Culture*
Kim Chan & Renée Mauborgne's *Blue Ocean Strategy*
Jared Diamond's *Guns, Germs & Steel: the Fate of Human Societies*
Jared Diamond's *Collapse: How Societies Choose to Fail or Survive*
E. E. Evans-Pritchard's *Witchcraft, Oracles and Magic Among the Azande*
James Ferguson's *The Anti-Politics Machine*
Clifford Geertz's *The Interpretation of Cultures*
David Graeber's *Debt: the First 5000 Years*
Karen Ho's *Liquidated: An Ethnography of Wall Street*
Geert Hofstede's *Culture's Consequences: Comparing Values, Behaviors, Institutes and Organizations across Nations*
Claude Lévi-Strauss's *Structural Anthropology*
Jay Macleod's *Ain't No Makin' It: Aspirations and Attainment in a Low-Income Neighborhood*
Saba Mahmood's *The Politics of Piety: The Islamic Revival and the Feminist Subject*
Marcel Mauss's *The Gift*

BUSINESS

Jean Lave & Etienne Wenger's *Situated Learning*
Theodore Levitt's *Marketing Myopia*
Burton G. Malkiel's *A Random Walk Down Wall Street*
Douglas McGregor's *The Human Side of Enterprise*
Michael Porter's *Competitive Strategy: Creating and Sustaining Superior Performance*
John Kotter's *Leading Change*
C. K. Prahalad & Gary Hamel's *The Core Competence of the Corporation*

CRIMINOLOGY

Michelle Alexander's *The New Jim Crow: Mass Incarceration in the Age of Colorblindness*
Michael R. Gottfredson & Travis Hirschi's *A General Theory of Crime*
Richard Herrnstein & Charles A. Murray's *The Bell Curve: Intelligence and Class Structure in American Life*
Elizabeth Loftus's *Eyewitness Testimony*
Jay Macleod's *Ain't No Makin' It: Aspirations and Attainment in a Low-Income Neighborhood*
Philip Zimbardo's *The Lucifer Effect*

ECONOMICS

Janet Abu-Lughod's *Before European Hegemony*
Ha-Joon Chang's *Kicking Away the Ladder*
David Brion Davis's *The Problem of Slavery in the Age of Revolution*
Milton Friedman's *The Role of Monetary Policy*
Milton Friedman's *Capitalism and Freedom*
David Graeber's *Debt: the First 5000 Years*
Friedrich Hayek's *The Road to Serfdom*
Karen Ho's *Liquidated: An Ethnography of Wall Street*

John Maynard Keynes's *The General Theory of Employment, Interest and Money*
Charles P. Kindleberger's *Manias, Panics and Crashes*
Robert Lucas's *Why Doesn't Capital Flow from Rich to Poor Countries?*
Burton G. Malkiel's *A Random Walk Down Wall Street*
Thomas Robert Malthus's *An Essay on the Principle of Population*
Karl Marx's *Capital*
Thomas Piketty's *Capital in the Twenty-First Century*
Amartya Sen's *Development as Freedom*
Adam Smith's *The Wealth of Nations*
Nassim Nicholas Taleb's *The Black Swan: The Impact of the Highly Improbable*
Amos Tversky's & Daniel Kahneman's *Judgment under Uncertainty: Heuristics and Biases*
Mahbub Ul Haq's *Reflections on Human Development*
Max Weber's *The Protestant Ethic and the Spirit of Capitalism*

FEMINISM AND GENDER STUDIES

Judith Butler's *Gender Trouble*
Simone De Beauvoir's *The Second Sex*
Michel Foucault's *History of Sexuality*
Betty Friedan's *The Feminine Mystique*
Saba Mahmood's *The Politics of Piety: The Islamic Revival and the Feminist Subject*
Joan Wallach Scott's *Gender and the Politics of History*
Mary Wollstonecraft's *A Vindication of the Rights of Woman*
Virginia Woolf's *A Room of One's Own*

GEOGRAPHY

The Brundtland Report's *Our Common Future*
Rachel Carson's *Silent Spring*
Charles Darwin's *On the Origin of Species*
James Ferguson's *The Anti-Politics Machine*
Jane Jacobs's *The Death and Life of Great American Cities*
James Lovelock's *Gaia: A New Look at Life on Earth*
Amartya Sen's *Development as Freedom*
Mathis Wackernagel & William Rees's *Our Ecological Footprint*

HISTORY

Janet Abu-Lughod's *Before European Hegemony*
Benedict Anderson's *Imagined Communities*
Bernard Bailyn's *The Ideological Origins of the American Revolution*
Hanna Batatu's *The Old Social Classes And The Revolutionary Movements Of Iraq*
Christopher Browning's *Ordinary Men: Reserve Police Batallion 101 and the Final Solution in Poland*
Edmund Burke's *Reflections on the Revolution in France*
William Cronon's *Nature's Metropolis: Chicago And The Great West*
Alfred W. Crosby's *The Columbian Exchange*
Hamid Dabashi's *Iran: A People Interrupted*
David Brion Davis's *The Problem of Slavery in the Age of Revolution*
Nathalie Zemon Davis's *The Return of Martin Guerre*
Jared Diamond's *Guns, Germs & Steel: the Fate of Human Societies*
Frank Dikotter's *Mao's Great Famine*
John W Dower's *War Without Mercy: Race And Power In The Pacific War*
W. E. B. Du Bois's *The Souls of Black Folk*
Richard J. Evans's *In Defence of History*
Lucien Febvre's *The Problem of Unbelief in the 16th Century*
Sheila Fitzpatrick's *Everyday Stalinism*

Eric Foner's *Reconstruction: America's Unfinished Revolution, 1863-1877*
Michel Foucault's *Discipline and Punish*
Michel Foucault's *History of Sexuality*
Francis Fukuyama's *The End of History and the Last Man*
John Lewis Gaddis's *We Now Know: Rethinking Cold War History*
Ernest Gellner's *Nations and Nationalism*
Eugene Genovese's *Roll, Jordan, Roll: The World the Slaves Made*
Carlo Ginzburg's *The Night Battles*
Daniel Goldhagen's *Hitler's Willing Executioners*
Jack Goldstone's *Revolution and Rebellion in the Early Modern World*
Antonio Gramsci's *The Prison Notebooks*
Alexander Hamilton, John Jay & James Madison's *The Federalist Papers*
Christopher Hill's *The World Turned Upside Down*
Carole Hillenbrand's *The Crusades: Islamic Perspectives*
Thomas Hobbes's *Leviathan*
Eric Hobsbawm's *The Age Of Revolution*
John A. Hobson's *Imperialism: A Study*
Albert Hourani's *History of the Arab Peoples*
Samuel P. Huntington's *The Clash of Civilizations and the Remaking of World Order*
C. L. R. James's *The Black Jacobins*
Tony Judt's *Postwar: A History of Europe Since 1945*
Ernst Kantorowicz's *The King's Two Bodies: A Study in Medieval Political Theology*
Paul Kennedy's *The Rise and Fall of the Great Powers*
Ian Kershaw's *The "Hitler Myth": Image and Reality in the Third Reich*
John Maynard Keynes's *The General Theory of Employment, Interest and Money*
Charles P. Kindleberger's *Manias, Panics and Crashes*
Martin Luther King Jr's *Why We Can't Wait*
Henry Kissinger's *World Order: Reflections on the Character of Nations and the Course of History*
Thomas Kuhn's *The Structure of Scientific Revolutions*
Georges Lefebvre's *The Coming of the French Revolution*
John Locke's *Two Treatises of Government*
Niccolò Machiavelli's *The Prince*
Thomas Robert Malthus's *An Essay on the Principle of Population*
Mahmood Mamdani's *Citizen and Subject: Contemporary Africa And The Legacy Of Late Colonialism*
Karl Marx's *Capital*
Stanley Milgram's *Obedience to Authority*
John Stuart Mill's *On Liberty*
Thomas Paine's *Common Sense*
Thomas Paine's *Rights of Man*
Geoffrey Parker's *Global Crisis: War, Climate Change and Catastrophe in the Seventeenth Century*
Jonathan Riley-Smith's *The First Crusade and the Idea of Crusading*
Jean-Jacques Rousseau's *The Social Contract*
Joan Wallach Scott's *Gender and the Politics of History*
Theda Skocpol's *States and Social Revolutions*
Adam Smith's *The Wealth of Nations*
Timothy Snyder's *Bloodlands: Europe Between Hitler and Stalin*
Sun Tzu's *The Art of War*
Keith Thomas's *Religion and the Decline of Magic*
Thucydides's *The History of the Peloponnesian War*
Frederick Jackson Turner's *The Significance of the Frontier in American History*
Odd Arne Westad's *The Global Cold War: Third World Interventions And The Making Of Our Times*

LITERATURE

Chinua Achebe's *An Image of Africa: Racism in Conrad's Heart of Darkness*
Roland Barthes's *Mythologies*
Homi K. Bhabha's *The Location of Culture*
Judith Butler's *Gender Trouble*
Simone De Beauvoir's *The Second Sex*
Ferdinand De Saussure's *Course in General Linguistics*
T. S. Eliot's *The Sacred Wood: Essays on Poetry and Criticism*
Zora Neale Huston's *Characteristics of Negro Expression*
Toni Morrison's *Playing in the Dark: Whiteness in the American Literary Imagination*
Edward Said's *Orientalism*
Gayatri Chakravorty Spivak's *Can the Subaltern Speak?*
Mary Wollstonecraft's *A Vindication of the Rights of Women*
Virginia Woolf's *A Room of One's Own*

PHILOSOPHY

Elizabeth Anscombe's *Modern Moral Philosophy*
Hannah Arendt's *The Human Condition*
Aristotle's *Metaphysics*
Aristotle's *Nicomachean Ethics*
Edmund Gettier's *Is Justified True Belief Knowledge?*
Georg Wilhelm Friedrich Hegel's *Phenomenology of Spirit*
David Hume's *Dialogues Concerning Natural Religion*
David Hume's *The Enquiry for Human Understanding*
Immanuel Kant's *Religion within the Boundaries of Mere Reason*
Immanuel Kant's *Critique of Pure Reason*
Søren Kierkegaard's *The Sickness Unto Death*
Søren Kierkegaard's *Fear and Trembling*
C. S. Lewis's *The Abolition of Man*
Alasdair MacIntyre's *After Virtue*
Marcus Aurelius's *Meditations*
Friedrich Nietzsche's *On the Genealogy of Morality*
Friedrich Nietzsche's *Beyond Good and Evil*
Plato's *Republic*
Plato's *Symposium*
Jean-Jacques Rousseau's *The Social Contract*
Gilbert Ryle's *The Concept of Mind*
Baruch Spinoza's *Ethics*
Sun Tzu's *The Art of War*
Ludwig Wittgenstein's *Philosophical Investigations*

POLITICS

Benedict Anderson's *Imagined Communities*
Aristotle's *Politics*
Bernard Bailyn's *The Ideological Origins of the American Revolution*
Edmund Burke's *Reflections on the Revolution in France*
John C. Calhoun's *A Disquisition on Government*
Ha-Joon Chang's *Kicking Away the Ladder*
Hamid Dabashi's *Iran: A People Interrupted*
Hamid Dabashi's *Theology of Discontent: The Ideological Foundation of the Islamic Revolution in Iran*
Robert Dahl's *Democracy and its Critics*
Robert Dahl's *Who Governs?*
David Brion Davis's *The Problem of Slavery in the Age of Revolution*

Alexis De Tocqueville's *Democracy in America*
James Ferguson's *The Anti-Politics Machine*
Frank Dikotter's *Mao's Great Famine*
Sheila Fitzpatrick's *Everyday Stalinism*
Eric Foner's *Reconstruction: America's Unfinished Revolution, 1863-1877*
Milton Friedman's *Capitalism and Freedom*
Francis Fukuyama's *The End of History and the Last Man*
John Lewis Gaddis's *We Now Know: Rethinking Cold War History*
Ernest Gellner's *Nations and Nationalism*
David Graeber's *Debt: the First 5000 Years*
Antonio Gramsci's *The Prison Notebooks*
Alexander Hamilton, John Jay & James Madison's *The Federalist Papers*
Friedrich Hayek's *The Road to Serfdom*
Christopher Hill's *The World Turned Upside Down*
Thomas Hobbes's *Leviathan*
John A. Hobson's *Imperialism: A Study*
Samuel P. Huntington's *The Clash of Civilizations and the Remaking of World Order*
Tony Judt's *Postwar: A History of Europe Since 1945*
David C. Kang's *China Rising: Peace, Power and Order in East Asia*
Paul Kennedy's *The Rise and Fall of Great Powers*
Robert Keohane's *After Hegemony*
Martin Luther King Jr.'s *Why We Can't Wait*
Henry Kissinger's *World Order: Reflections on the Character of Nations and the Course of History*
John Locke's *Two Treatises of Government*
Niccolò Machiavelli's *The Prince*
Thomas Robert Malthus's *An Essay on the Principle of Population*
Mahmood Mamdani's *Citizen and Subject: Contemporary Africa And The Legacy Of Late Colonialism*
Karl Marx's *Capital*
John Stuart Mill's *On Liberty*
John Stuart Mill's *Utilitarianism*
Hans Morgenthau's *Politics Among Nations*
Thomas Paine's *Common Sense*
Thomas Paine's *Rights of Man*
Thomas Piketty's *Capital in the Twenty-First Century*
Robert D. Putman's *Bowling Alone*
John Rawls's *Theory of Justice*
Jean-Jacques Rousseau's *The Social Contract*
Theda Skocpol's *States and Social Revolutions*
Adam Smith's *The Wealth of Nations*
Sun Tzu's *The Art of War*
Henry David Thoreau's *Civil Disobedience*
Thucydides's *The History of the Peloponnesian War*
Kenneth Waltz's *Theory of International Politics*
Max Weber's *Politics as a Vocation*
Odd Arne Westad's *The Global Cold War: Third World Interventions And The Making Of Our Times*

POSTCOLONIAL STUDIES

Roland Barthes's *Mythologies*
Frantz Fanon's *Black Skin, White Masks*
Homi K. Bhabha's *The Location of Culture*
Gustavo Gutiérrez's *A Theology of Liberation*
Edward Said's *Orientalism*
Gayatri Chakravorty Spivak's *Can the Subaltern Speak?*

PSYCHOLOGY

Gordon Allport's *The Nature of Prejudice*
Alan Baddeley & Graham Hitch's *Aggression: A Social Learning Analysis*
Albert Bandura's *Aggression: A Social Learning Analysis*
Leon Festinger's *A Theory of Cognitive Dissonance*
Sigmund Freud's *The Interpretation of Dreams*
Betty Friedan's *The Feminine Mystique*
Michael R. Gottfredson & Travis Hirschi's *A General Theory of Crime*
Eric Hoffer's *The True Believer: Thoughts on the Nature of Mass Movements*
William James's *Principles of Psychology*
Elizabeth Loftus's *Eyewitness Testimony*
A. H. Maslow's *A Theory of Human Motivation*
Stanley Milgram's *Obedience to Authority*
Steven Pinker's *The Better Angels of Our Nature*
Oliver Sacks's *The Man Who Mistook His Wife For a Hat*
Richard Thaler & Cass Sunstein's *Nudge: Improving Decisions About Health, Wealth and Happiness*
Amos Tversky's *Judgment under Uncertainty: Heuristics and Biases*
Philip Zimbardo's *The Lucifer Effect*

SCIENCE

Rachel Carson's *Silent Spring*
William Cronon's *Nature's Metropolis: Chicago And The Great West*
Alfred W. Crosby's *The Columbian Exchange*
Charles Darwin's *On the Origin of Species*
Richard Dawkin's *The Selfish Gene*
Thomas Kuhn's *The Structure of Scientific Revolutions*
Geoffrey Parker's *Global Crisis: War, Climate Change and Catastrophe in the Seventeenth Century*
Mathis Wackernagel & William Rees's *Our Ecological Footprint*

SOCIOLOGY

Michelle Alexander's *The New Jim Crow: Mass Incarceration in the Age of Colorblindness*
Gordon Allport's *The Nature of Prejudice*
Albert Bandura's *Aggression: A Social Learning Analysis*
Hanna Batatu's *The Old Social Classes And The Revolutionary Movements Of Iraq*
Ha-Joon Chang's *Kicking Away the Ladder*
W. E. B. Du Bois's *The Souls of Black Folk*
Émile Durkheim's *On Suicide*
Frantz Fanon's *Black Skin, White Masks*
Frantz Fanon's *The Wretched of the Earth*
Eric Foner's *Reconstruction: America's Unfinished Revolution, 1863-1877*
Eugene Genovese's *Roll, Jordan, Roll: The World the Slaves Made*
Jack Goldstone's *Revolution and Rebellion in the Early Modern World*
Antonio Gramsci's *The Prison Notebooks*
Richard Herrnstein & Charles A Murray's *The Bell Curve: Intelligence and Class Structure in American Life*
Eric Hoffer's *The True Believer: Thoughts on the Nature of Mass Movements*
Jane Jacobs's *The Death and Life of Great American Cities*
Robert Lucas's *Why Doesn't Capital Flow from Rich to Poor Countries?*
Jay Macleod's *Ain't No Makin' It: Aspirations and Attainment in a Low Income Neighborhood*
Elaine May's *Homeward Bound: American Families in the Cold War Era*
Douglas McGregor's *The Human Side of Enterprise*
C. Wright Mills's *The Sociological Imagination*

Thomas Piketty's *Capital in the Twenty-First Century*
Robert D. Putman's *Bowling Alone*
David Riesman's *The Lonely Crowd: A Study of the Changing American Character*
Edward Said's *Orientalism*
Joan Wallach Scott's *Gender and the Politics of History*
Theda Skocpol's *States and Social Revolutions*
Max Weber's *The Protestant Ethic and the Spirit of Capitalism*

THEOLOGY

Augustine's *Confessions*
Benedict's *Rule of St Benedict*
Gustavo Gutiérrez's *A Theology of Liberation*
Carole Hillenbrand's *The Crusades: Islamic Perspectives*
David Hume's *Dialogues Concerning Natural Religion*
Immanuel Kant's *Religion within the Boundaries of Mere Reason*
Ernst Kantorowicz's *The King's Two Bodies: A Study in Medieval Political Theology*
Søren Kierkegaard's *The Sickness Unto Death*
C. S. Lewis's *The Abolition of Man*
Saba Mahmood's *The Politics of Piety: The Islamic Revival and the Feminist Subject*
Baruch Spinoza's *Ethics*
Keith Thomas's *Religion and the Decline of Magic*

COMING SOON

Chris Argyris's *The Individual and the Organisation*
Seyla Benhabib's *The Rights of Others*
Walter Benjamin's *The Work Of Art in the Age of Mechanical Reproduction*
John Berger's *Ways of Seeing*
Pierre Bourdieu's *Outline of a Theory of Practice*
Mary Douglas's *Purity and Danger*
Roland Dworkin's *Taking Rights Seriously*
James G. March's *Exploration and Exploitation in Organisational Learning*
Ikujiro Nonaka's *A Dynamic Theory of Organizational Knowledge Creation*
Griselda Pollock's *Vision and Difference*
Amartya Sen's *Inequality Re-Examined*
Susan Sontag's *On Photography*
Yasser Tabbaa's *The Transformation of Islamic Art*
Ludwig von Mises's *Theory of Money and Credit*

Macat Pairs

Analyse historical and modern issues from opposite sides of an argument. Pairs include:

INTERNATIONAL RELATIONS IN THE 21ST CENTURY

Samuel P. Huntington's
The Clash of Civilisations
In his highly influential 1996 book, Huntington offers a vision of a post-Cold War world in which conflict takes place not between competing ideologies but between cultures. The worst clash, he argues, will be between the Islamic world and the West: the West's arrogance and belief that its culture is a "gift" to the world will come into conflict with Islam's obstinacy and concern that its culture is under attack from a morally decadent "other."

Clash inspired much debate between different political schools of thought. But its greatest impact came in helping define American foreign policy in the wake of the 2001 terrorist attacks in New York and Washington.

Francis Fukuyama's
The End of History and the Last Man
Published in 1992, *The End of History and the Last Man* argues that capitalist democracy is the final destination for all societies. Fukuyama believed democracy triumphed during the Cold War because it lacks the "fundamental contradictions" inherent in communism and satisfies our yearning for freedom and equality. Democracy therefore marks the endpoint in the evolution of ideology, and so the "end of history." There will still be "events," but no fundamental change in ideology.

Macat analyses are available from all good bookshops and libraries.

Access hundreds of analyses through one, multimedia tool.
Join free for one month **library.macat.com**

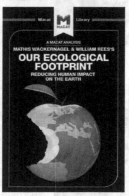

Macat Pairs

*Analyse historical and modern issues from opposite sides of an argument.
Pairs include:*

ARE WE FUNDAMENTALLY GOOD - OR BAD?

Steven Pinker's
The Better Angels of Our Nature
Stephen Pinker's gloriously optimistic 2011 book argues that, despite humanity's biological tendency toward violence, we are, in fact, less violent today than ever before. To prove his case, Pinker lays out pages of detailed statistical evidence. For him, much of the credit for the decline goes to the eighteenth-century Enlightenment movement, whose ideas of liberty, tolerance, and respect for the value of human life filtered down through society and affected how people thought. That psychological change led to behavioral change—and overall we became more peaceful. Critics countered that humanity could never overcome the biological urge toward violence; others argued that Pinker's statistics were flawed.

Philip Zimbardo's
The Lucifer Effect
Some psychologists believe those who commit cruelty are innately evil. Zimbardo disagrees. In *The Lucifer Effect*, he argues that sometimes good people do evil things simply because of the situations they find themselves in, citing many historical examples to illustrate his point. Zimbardo details his 1971 Stanford prison experiment, where ordinary volunteers playing guards in a mock prison rapidly became abusive. But he also describes the tortures committed by US army personnel in Iraq's Abu Ghraib prison in 2003—and how he himself testified in defence of one of those guards. committed by US army personnel in Iraq's Abu Ghraib prison in 2003—and how he himself testified in defence of one of those guards.

Macat Pairs

*Analyse historical and modern issues
from opposite sides of an argument.
Pairs include:*

HOW WE RELATE TO EACH OTHER AND SOCIETY

Jean-Jacques Rousseau's
The Social Contract

Rousseau's famous work sets out the radical concept of the 'social contract': a give-and-take relationship between individual freedom and social order.

If people are free to do as they like, governed only by their own sense of justice, they are also vulnerable to chaos and violence. To avoid this, Rousseau proposes, they should agree to give up some freedom to benefit from the protection of social and political organization. But this deal is only just if societies are led by the collective needs and desires of the people, and able to control the private interests of individuals. For Rousseau, the only legitimate form of government is rule by the people.

Robert D. Putnam's
Bowling Alone

In *Bowling Alone*, Robert Putnam argues that Americans have become disconnected from one another and from the institutions of their common life, and investigates the consequences of this change.

Looking at a range of indicators, from membership in formal organizations to the number of invitations being extended to informal dinner parties, Putnam demonstrates that Americans are interacting less and creating less "social capital" – with potentially disastrous implications for their society.

It would be difficult to overstate the impact of *Bowling Alone*, one of the most frequently cited social science publications of the last half-century.

Macat analyses are available from all good bookshops and libraries.

Access hundreds of analyses through one, multimedia tool.
Join free for one month **library.macat.com**

Printed in the United States
by Baker & Taylor Publisher Services